Congress Confronts the Court

CONGRESS CONFRONTS THE COURT

THE STRUGGLE FOR LEGITIMACY AND AUTHORITY IN LAWMAKING

edited by

COLTON C. CAMPBELL
and JOHN F. STACK JR.

ROWMAN & LITTLEFIELD PUBLISHERS, INC.
Lanham • Boulder • New York • Oxford

ROWMAN & LITTLEFIELD PUBLISHERS, INC.

Published in the United States of America
by Rowman & Littlefield Publishers, Inc.
4720 Boston Way, Lanham, Maryland 20706
www.rowmanlittlefield.com

12 Hid's Copse Road, Cumnor Hill, Oxford OX2 9JJ, England

British Library Cataloguing in Publication Information Available

Library of Congress Cataloging-in-Publication Data

Congress confronts the court : the struggle for legitimacy and authority in lawmaking /
edited by Colton C. Campbell and John F. Stack Jr.
    p. cm.
    Includes bibliographical references and index.
    ISBN 0-7425-0138-8 (alk. paper)—ISBN 0-7425-0139-6 (pbk. : alk. paper)
    1. Political questions and judicial power—United States. 2. Legislation—United
States. 3. United States—Politics and government—1993– I. Campbell, Colton C.,
1965– II. Stack, John F.

    KF8748 .C565 2001
    328.73'07453—dc21   00-059054

Printed in the United States of America

♾™ The paper used in this publication meets the minimum requirements of American
National Standard for Information Sciences—Permanence of Paper for Printed Library
Materials, ANSI/NISO Z39.48-1992.

For our mothers,

Ardis Jones Campbell

and

Margaret Mahoney Stack,

strong-minded, independent, indefatigable women

Contents

Tables

Illustrations

Preface

Former Senator Howard Baker of Tennessee once remarked that government should always be a part of the solution not a part of the problem. As this book goes to press, Senator Baker's words have a particular relevance. Congress, the federal courts, and the executive branch illustrate the difficulty of formulating national public policy and fairly enforcing such choices. Attorney General Janet Reno's wrenching decision to return young Elián González to the custody of his father on Saturday, April 22, 2000, underscores this delicate balance. Notwithstanding the outrage of many Cuban Americans in Miami, that determination underscores the fundamental importance of the rule of law and, as important, its neutral enforcement in American society.

In large measure, this book is about how Congress and the Supreme Court work to define their lawmaking functions. This is a highly dynamic process sometimes overlooked by those who conceptualize these branches in purely formal terms. Just as Elián González's custody battle reflects different conceptions of the role of politics, ideology, self-interest, and pressure group politics, so too does the relationship between Congress and the Court under the Constitution.

The contributions to this volume document Congress's relations with the Court and the Court's understanding of congressional prerogatives as they change over time. The Constitution grants to both branches surprising fluidity in interpreting their roles, which reveals the importance of a government based on law, capable of conflict, change, and reevaluation over time. Chief Justice John Marshall declared in *Marbury v. Madison* (1803) that the Constitution is paramount. Within this ingenious political framework both Congress and the Supreme Court have more maneuverability than traditional assessments might suggest.

As with any collaborative enterprise, this book would not have been possible without the cooperation of many individuals. We must first thank our academic colleagues who participated in the project. Particular gratitude should be given to our departmental colleagues, Mary Beth Melchior, Keith Dougherty, and Lui Hebron, who graciously indulged us in yet another project on Congress. We also extend special thanks to three of our finest graduate students, David Twigg, Eric Nemiroff, and Samia Harb, whose involvement enriched the quality of the book.

Once again, the Jack D. Gordon Institute for Public Policy and Citizenship Studies made enormous contributions. Provost Mark B. Rosenberg's support and encouragement is especially appreciated. We gratefully acknowledge the contributions of Dr. Thomas Breslin, vice president of research; Dr. Arthur Herriot, dean of the college of arts and sciences; and Dr. Ivelaw L. Griffith, associate dean of the college of arts and sciences at Florida International University.

We especially acknowledge the intellectual contributions of Dr. Nicol Rae, chair of the department of political science, as a student of American politics and his understanding of the role of Congress, therein. Elaine Dillashaw of the Gordon Institute provided invaluable support and assistance. We are also indebted to Gail Galloway, Eileen Colton, and Nicholette Smith in the Supreme Court Curator's Office as well as to Heather Moore, the Senate photo historian, for providing the photos that appear throughout this book. To all these individuals and groups, we express our deepest appreciation.

CCC   JFS
Ukiah, Calif.   *Miami, Fla.*

Congress Confronts the Court

CHAPTER ONE

Diverging Perspectives on Lawmaking: The Delicate Balance between Congress and the Court

COLTON C. CAMPBELL AND JOHN F. STACK JR.

The formal institutional ties between Congress and the Supreme Court are complex and interdependent. Congress seeks a judicial system that faithfully construes the laws of the legislative branch and efficiently discharges them, whereas the judiciary seeks an environment respectful of its independence (Katzmann 1997). In the end, the relationship between Congress and the Court is critical to the legitimacy and administration of justice.

Congressional–judicial relations are neither static nor unidimensional. History, circumstance, political struggles, and the articulation of issues by Congress and the Court drive the delicate balance among lawmaking functions. For too long, the Supreme Court has been studied as an isolated entity, void of politics, that reaches judgments by some unseen and unknowable logic (Brigham 1987). Likewise, Congress is commonly approached as a singularly political enterprise with little regard for its nuanced lawmaking and lawgiving functions. This is ironic, since as early as 1789, Congress defined the scope and jurisdiction of the federal court system as established under article III of the Constitution. Such legislative precedent helped lay the foundation for a sometime stormy relationship between Congress and the Court.

Our intent is to highlight some of the missing elements involved in congressional–judicial relations. While the Constitution establishes three branches of government, each with distinctively shared functions, no one branch acts alone. As the chapters that follow illustrate, the overlap between Congress and the Court is dynamic, far-reaching, and ongoing. It is a struggle for institutional balance that frequently shifts with the politics of the moment—politics that are themselves reflections of the search for institutional equilibrium.

1

The photos and drawing that follow illustrate the three permanent homes of the Supreme Court. Photo 1.1 shows the old Supreme Court chamber in the United States Capitol, where the Court sat from 1810 to 1860. When the Capitol was built, no room was provided for the Supreme Court and hence the courtroom was placed in the basement of the Capitol. By 1860 the Supreme Court moved into the old Senate chamber in the U.S. Capitol. Here the Court sat between 1860 and 1935 (photo 1.2). The last two photos show the Court's new quarters—the Supreme Court building's front grand façade constructed in 1936 (photo 1.3) and the Supreme Court chamber as it appeared in 1990 (figure 1.1)—far removed from the humble courtroom in the basement of the Capitol building. By the time of Franklin D. Roosevelt's election as president in 1932, the Supreme Court had established itself unequivocally as a coequal branch of government.

CONGRESS AND THE COURT: TOWARD INSTITUTIONAL COMITY

The Constitution deliberately engenders institutional competition and cooperation between the two branches. Historical patterns and individual attitudes have deviated among conflict, compromise, and acquiescence, along with episodic periods of activism and restraint. Nominations of individuals to serve in the federal judiciary must be approved with the "advice and consent" of the Senate. Congress balances or stacks the courts through the creation of judgeships (De Figueiredo and Tiller 1996); it determines the structure, jurisdiction, procedures, and substantive law of the federal courts (Kay 1981; Rice 1981; Rossum 1983; Gunther 1984); it passes laws affecting such disparate areas as judicial discipline and sentencing policy; and it sets appropriations and compensation (Yarwood and Canon 1980; Toma 1991; Katzmann 1997). The Court affects Congress whenever justices construe the meaning of the Constitution, treaties, federal statutes, administrative agencies, and the decisions of federal and state courts.

Although the legislative and judicial branches share an affinity—prevalence of legal training—generalizations about their interaction are especially difficult to pin down. Structural, procedural, and perceptual differences affect such institutional interchange as well as divergent career paths (Davidson 1988). This relationship is strained by an array of issues: a congested judicial caseload, federalization of the law, resource constraints, concerns about the confirmation process, increasing legislative scrutiny of judicial decision making, and the administration of justice (Katzmann 1997) as well as debates about how courts should interpret legislation (U.S. Congress, Joint Committee on the Organization of Congress 1993).

Early accounts of congressional–judicial relations often accepted the notion that the Court was protected from legislative attack by an aura of reverence to justices (Schmidhauser and Berg 1972). But lawmakers have long supported

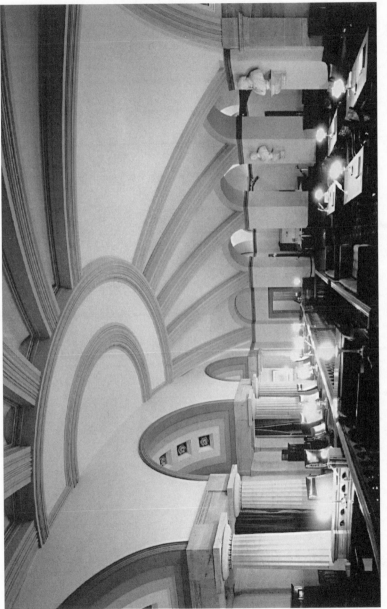

Photo 1.1   The Old Supreme Court Chamber (U.S. Capitol), where the Court sat from 1810 to 1860. Photo taken by Franz Jantzen, collection of the Supreme Court of the United States

Photo 1.2 The Old Senate Chamber (U.S. Capitol), where the Court sat from 1860 to 1935. Photographer unknown, collection of the Supreme Court of the United States

Photo 1.3   Photograph of the full west elevation of the Supreme Court, taken in 1993. Photo taken by Franz Jantzen, collection of the Supreme Court of the United States

Figure 1.1   The Supreme Court Chamber in 1990

Source: J. Floyd Yewell, artist, collection of the Supreme Court of the United States.

proposals to reverse various facets of policies made by justices and even to curb the Court's basic authority (Nagel 1962; Stumpf 1965; Berger 1969; Breckenridge 1970; Schmidhauser and Berg 1972; Brest 1986; Mikva and Bleich 1991). Conversation turns to confrontation whenever representatives and senators or mobilized segments of their constituencies disapprove of specific decisions by the High Bench, or when those officials fear that their own policymaking prerogatives are being threatened (Murphy 1962).

In the 1950s and 1960s congressional antagonism occurred when legislators charged the Warren Court (1953–1969) with taking untenable positions and engaging in unjustified activism (Baum 1992). These rulings entailed the selective incorporation of a number of provisions within the first ten amendments of the Constitution, the Bill of Rights: the outlawing of prayer in public schools (*Engel v. Vitale* [1962]); the right to counsel in all felony cases (*Gideon v. Wainwright* [1963]); the right to privacy (*Griswold v. Connecticut* [1965]); and the right to trial by jury when serious crime is involved (*Duncan v. Louisiana* [1968]).

Typical of congressional criticism that justices received during this period were Senator Barry Goldwater's (R-Ariz.) statements that the Court had "ruled against God" as well as the remarks of other legislators to the effect that the Court had no business taking God out of the public schools (quoted in Ducat 2000, 1115). This culminated in denunciations of the Court, especially in the south, with calls to impeach Chief Justice Earl Warren.

Interbranch conflict also occurs when the Court picks up the pieces that Congress has left scattered. Members of Congress and their staff aides will not remain silent as their legislative products are reshaped and adjusted in the judicial arena (Davidson 1988). They may play roles of lobbyists or claimants, calling upon the legislative record they have created to buttress their interpretations. Or they may stand on the sidelines, waiting for the Court to reach difficult decisions that have been blurred by the lawmakers (Davidson 1988, 116).

As the product of an English-based judicial system, the Supreme Court is bound to honor the concept of stare decisis—adherence to previously decided precedent. This emphasis on law made by a judge provides the Court with exceptional power in the American constitutional system. As Chief Justice John Marshall writing for a unanimous Supreme Court held in *Marbury v. Madison* (1803), courts interpret the law. Even within the common law's deference to precedent, courts can and do construe statutes, precedent, the facts of cases, and legislation in such ways as to fashion new law. As many of the chapters in this volume suggest, sea changes—unanticipated, even radical departures from traditional approaches to constitutional interpretation—occur with some regularity in American law.

In recent years Congress has increasingly asserted its institutional prerogatives in its dealings with the Court over a number of issues. In the now tortuous

Photo 1.4   The Warren Court in 1966. Photo taken by Ackad, collection of the Supreme Court of the United States

confirmation process of judicial nominations, for example, the legislative branch has stifled a number of judicial appointments to the bench (Davidson and Campbell forthcoming). Senators routinely question nominees about the way they approach statutes, making clear their displeasure with legal reasoning that disregards legislative history (Katzmann 1997). Lawmakers confront the redistricting of House seats from the perspective of how census tracts are developed and computed. This has been in response to the Court's invalidation of many congressional majority–minority districts as being racial or ethnic gerrymanders in violation of the Fourteenth Amendment Equal Protection Clause (Durbin 1996).

In areas of criminal law enforcement, religious rights, reproductive rights, and such First Amendment issues as pornography on the Internet and gay and lesbian rights, legislative action is both assertive and ideologically opposed to judicial review. Tables 1.1 and 1.2 illustrate the range of recent congressional action aimed at thwarting Supreme Court decisions. In most respects, the politics of congressional response to the Court's invalidation of federal law resembles congressional politics generally (Eskridge 1991; Solimine and Walker 1992; Baum 1998), and the Court generally acquiesces (Biskupic and Witt 1997). Some overrides follow soon after a

TABLE 1.1 SELECTED LEGISLATION OVERTURNING SUPREME COURT STATUTORY DECISIONS

Migrant Worker Protection (enacted 1995)
Overturned *Adams Fruit Co. v. Barret* (1990) by not allowing migrant farm workers from suing employers for injuries when they could obtain workers' compensation benefits for those injuries.

False Statements Accountability Act of 1996
Overturned *Hubbard v. United States* (1995) by making it a criminal offense to make a false statement in a judicial proceeding.

Federal Courts Improvement Act of 1996
Overturned *Pulliam v. Allen* (1984) by giving judges immunity from lawsuits for injunctive relief and from the payment of costs in lawsuits; also overturned *Primate Protection League v. Administrators of Tulane Educational Fund* (1991) by allowing federal agencies to remove lawsuits against them from state to federal court.

Small Business Job Protection Act of 1996
Partially overturned *John Hancock Mutual Life Insurance v. Harris Trust* (1993) by providing life insurance companies an exemption from federal pension regulations for certain funds until 1999.

110 Stat. 3009-369, sec. 657, 1996
Overturned *United States v. Lopez* (1995) by banning handguns in local school zones.

Source: Adapted from Lawrence Baum, *The Supreme Court*, 6th ed. (Washington, D.C.: Congressional Quarterly, 1998).

TABLE 1.2 SELECTED RESOLUTIONS INTRODUCED IN CONGRESS FOR CONSTITUTIONAL AMENDMENTS TO OVERTURN SUPREME COURT DECISIONS

Purpose	Decisions Overturned
Ongoing attempts to prohibit international compacts (executive agreements) other than treaties from becoming effective as international law in the United States without an act of Congress	*United States v. Belmont* (1937)
Giving states power to impose term limits on members of Congress	*U.S. Term Limits v. Thornton* (1995)
Giving Congress power to limit campaign spending	*Buckley v. Valeo* (1976)
Permitting organized prayer in public schools	*Engel v. Vitale* (1962)
Providing federal and state governments power to prohibit flag desecration	*Texas v. Johnson* (1989) *United States v. Eichman* (1990)
Prohibiting abortion under most circumstances	*Roe v. Wade* (1973) *Planned Parenthood v. Casey* (1992)
Enabling states to reduce prisoners' credits toward early release retroactively	*Lynce v. Mathis* (1997)

Source: Adapted from Lawrence Baum, *The Supreme Court*, 6th ed. (Washington, D.C.: Congressional Quarterly, 1998).

decision, while others come considerably later. In many cases, lawmakers are constrained by the lobbying efforts of beneficiaries of the Court's rulings (O'Brien 1995). Still, Congress regularly reviews and challenges the decisions of the Supreme Court; the High Bench does not exist in an apolitical vacuum.

From a selective survey of successful and failed attempts by Congress to override Supreme Court judgments, Eskridge (1991) finds that congressional committees carefully monitor Supreme Court decisions. Lawmakers are particularly prone to override decisions that reflect a closely divided Court favoring conservative interpretations; decisions that rely on the statute's plain meaning and canons of statutory construction; and judgments that reject positions taken by federal, state, and local governments (Eskridge 1991). The Civil Rights Act of 1991, for instance, reversed twelve rulings of the Court. Between 1967 and 1990, Congress overrode 121 of the Court's statutory decisions. In contrast, between 1945 and 1957 Congress overrode only twenty-one rulings (O'Brien 1995). Moreover, Congress has increasingly overruled lower federal court decisions.

O'Brien (1995, 1190) indicates that 73 percent of the decisions overturned were handed down by the Court less than ten years earlier. Almost 40 percent were conservative rulings while 20 percent were liberal holdings, and in slightly over 40 percent there was no clear liberal–conservative split (O'Brien 1995). The decisions reversed by Congress most commonly involved civil rights, followed by criminal law, antitrust law, bankruptcy, federal jurisdiction, and environmental law. In sum, on major issues of public policy, Congress is likely to predominate or at least to temper the impact of the Supreme Court's rulings and its exercise of judicial review.

Assessment of the seemingly new activism between the legislative and judicial branches should be placed within both the historical and policy-related frameworks of the past two decades. For example, addressing such questions as: Do the increasing tensions between Congress and the Court represent a new reassertion of legislative power at the expense of judicial review? What are the cumulative effects of sustained partisan politics since the 1980s? How have both institutions confronted deep partisan divisions over the past two decades that may have created a new institutional setting as defined by hostility to Supreme Court activism in the 1950s, 1960s, and 1990s?

LEGISLATIVE SCRUTINY OF JUDICIAL NOMINEES

No example better illustrates the tension between Congress and the Court than the increasing senatorial scrutiny of judicial nominees to federal judgeships. No federal judge can be seated without having been confirmed by a majority vote of the Senate. Although congressional cooperation in appointments is more the rule than the exception (Fisher 1997), senators are increasingly prepared to exploit this unique prerogative. Some senators routinely take advantage of their leverage to thwart nominations if they consider the nominees are out of step with existing congressional majorities (Lewis 1997; Peterson 1998). Others regard advice and consent not as a mere formality but as an important means of exercising continuing control over the federal judiciary.

Today's appointment process is much more formal and structured, longer—often more than many months longer—and more visible and consistently contentious than ever, according to the Twentieth Century Fund (now The Century Foundation) Task Force on the Presidential Appointment Process (Mackenzie and Shogan 1996, 37). The confirmation hearings themselves, along with interest-group lobbying and media coverage, are all part of today's landscape. Photo 1.5 illustrates how the Senate confirmation process was qualitatively easier during the late 1930s. Here, Dean Acheson, counsel for Supreme Court nominee Felix Frankfurter, listens to testimony opposing his client's appointment to the High Bench by George E. Sullivan, Washington attorney and author. Sullivan opposed Frankfurter's nomination on the grounds that Frankfurter was alien born (in Austria) and that he had alien affiliations. The Senate, nonetheless, successfully confirmed Frankfurter.

Photo 1.5   Senate confirmation hearing of Felix Frankfurter, January 10, 1939. Photo taken by Harris and Ewing, collection of the Supreme Court of the United States

One scholar observes how the Senate confirmation process has evolved in the last seventy-five years of the twentieth century in approximately three phases (Katzmann 1997, 19): 1922 to 1955, when senators infrequently questioned nominees; 1955 to 1967, when nominees' appearances before the Senate Judiciary Committee became a routine part of the confirmation process; and 1987 to the present, in which hearings have become occasions for conflict and grandstanding.

In the area of judicial nominations, senatorial prerogative and privilege are critically important. While the federal judiciary is overwhelmingly the creation of Congress, the nomination of judges is the unique preserve of the United States Senate. The executive branch nominates candidates for the federal judiciary but the Senate determines who shall serve. Shared responsibility means, according to Katzmann (1997, 12), the commitment by Congress and the presidency to maintain a strong and independent Court. A strong presumption in favor of deference to presidential prerogative to fill vacancies on the Supreme Court existed for most of this century (Silverstein 1994). Judicial nominees were expected to exhibit a nominal level of competence as well as possess political perspectives that worked within the sometimes narrow constraints of American politics (Silverstein 1994, 4). The Senate typically confirmed judicial nominees by a voice vote without record opposition.

The appointment of judicial nominees has also become part of a process of senatorial assertiveness in terms of both the federal judiciary and the executive branch. Senators increasingly use their advice and consent power to be heard (Horn 1993), sometimes pressing for their own political objectives. Candidates for federally appointed judgeships are routinely questioned about their legal, personal, and professional credentials as well as their activities as public and private figures. Senatorial scrutiny also encompasses a range of social and political concerns, the candidates' understanding of the Constitution, assessment of federal court decisions, ongoing constitutional controversies, partisan considerations, and statements of judicial philosophy (Rutkus 1994). More often than not, judicial nominees are embroiled in the appointment process—a far cry from the time when nominees were nearly completely removed from the political process. The judicial appointment process has become the new hot seat for nominees, whereby a nominee's demeanor, responsiveness, and knowledge of the law may well be critical in determining whether the Senate votes favorably.

It remains unclear at what point during the confirmation hearing itself that a nominee can or should decline to answer questions posed by members of the Senate Judiciary Committee (Rutkus 1993). When senators probe nominees on a variety of legal and constitutional matters, nominees risk compromising their future judicial independence by offering overly solicitous responses to ensure their confirmation (Rutkus 1994). Nominees also worry that forthright responses to any number of queries might vex senators with divergent ideological and partisan perspectives and thus jeopardize their confirmation. When the nominee is relatively controversial or is perceived by committee members to be evasive or insincere in responding to certain questions, lengthy questioning, occurring over several days of the hearing, is likely (Rutkus 1994; Krutz, Fleisher, and Bond 1998).

Senate confirmation hearings are also an important vehicle by which senators attempt to shed light on the character and fitness of the nominee to serve on the federal bench. In 1992 the Senate Judiciary Committee instituted the practice of conducting a closed-door session with each Supreme Court nominee to address any questions about the nominee's background which confidential investigations might have brought to the committee's attention (Rutkus 1994). In announcing this procedure, Senator Joseph R. Biden (D-Del.), who was chairman of the committee at that time, explained that such hearings would be conducted "in all cases, even when there are no major investigative issues to be resolved so that the holding of such a hearing cannot be taken to demonstrate that the committee has received adverse confidential information about the nomination" (quoted in Rutkus 1994, 6).

The grueling process of judicial confirmations has dramatically reduced the number of federal judicial positions to be filled (Light 2000). Lawmakers may undermine the influence of potentially opposing judges and concentrate within the judiciary a core of judges with a political ideology consistent with their preferences (De Figueiredo and Tiller 1996). Legislative majorities then enjoy the benefits of having a judiciary in place that will ensure that their policies are achieved in court, thereby relieving Congress of costly intervention (De Figueiredo and Tiller 1996).

THE CONTRIBUTING CHAPTERS

The remainder of the book is divided into three sections. Part one addresses legislative awareness of and responsiveness to judicial decisions. The common belief that the Supreme Court is the ultimate and final arbiter of constitutional law is challenged: lawmaking functions often seen as the sole prerogative of the judiciary are continually checked and guided by Congress. Part two assesses new sources of congressional–judicial tension. Here, the judicial activism of the Supreme Court is assessed in terms of its impact on Congress and other institutions. Part three concludes the volume with an overview of how Congress and the Court operate in the context of American political institutions.

In chapter two, "Congressional Checks on the Judiciary," Louis Fisher posits that the conventional view of judicial supremacy is a far more dynamic and less hierarchical model than contemporary wisdom supposes. Especially during the twentieth century, Congress sometimes aggressively challenged the Supreme Court's interpretation of the Constitution and federal law. Decisions by the Court are frequently defined by other political institutions at both federal and state levels. As early as 1832 President Andrew Jackson asserted the power of the president to independently analyze legislation presented to him regardless of judicial interpretation. Throughout the nineteenth and twentieth centuries, Congress repeatedly enacted laws overturning Supreme Court decisions.

In chapter three, "Separation of Powers and Judicial Impeachment," Mary L. Volcansek illustrates how both Congress and the presidency regularly influence judicial decision making, short of the most extreme sanction—impeachment. For example, through its investigatory powers (law enforcement agencies) the executive can provide lawmakers with a case for impeachment without first bringing criminal charges. The very threat of impeachment or press reports of embarrassing information about a federal judge's alleged misconduct may serve as a powerful inducement for a change of behavior and/or a push toward retirement for a particular federal judge. In short, courts do not have the last say and the executive branch plays an important (if unseen) role in a process often viewed as the sole preserve of Congress and the Supreme Court.

Chapter four, "Congress and the Court: The Strange Case of Census 2000," by Thomas L. Brunell, examines the fierce, partisan politics waged over the constitutionally mandated census process. For almost a decade, members of Congress sought to accurately count the nation's population. To this end, the Decennial Census Improvement Act of 1991 adjusted the census results to reduce the undercounting of children, minorities, and the poor, very much in the interest of the Democratic majority that controlled the House at that time. However, by 1997, the Republican-controlled Congress enacted new legislation stopping the use of Democratic sampling techniques, an effort subsequently vetoed by President Clinton. The Supreme Court settled the controversy in *Department of Commerce v. U.S. House of Representatives* (1999) by striking down the use of statistical sampling to measure population shifts. Because congressional districts are crafted by state legislatures every ten years according to population gains or losses, reapportionment is a major vehicle for enhancing or diminishing a political party's electoral fortunes on Capitol Hill.

In chapter five, "How the Republican War Over 'Judicial Activism' Has Cost Congress," David M. O'Brien approaches the flip side of congressional–judicial relations, with an assessment of how the Supreme Court, led by Chief Justice William Rehnquist, has sought to curb legislative power. Central to this thesis is that a realignment of congressional–judicial relations, and changing constitutional boundaries between congressional and state powers, is at work. Republican presidents and members of Congress have turned federal judgeships into instruments of partisan political power, thereby imposing greater ideological standards in the judicial selection process. The result has been a polarization of politics as the Senate considers nominees to federal judicial appointments.

Chapter six, "Congress, the Court, and Religious Liberty: The Case of *Employment Division of Oregon v. Smith*," by Carolyn N. Long, examines in detail the tug-of-war between the Supreme Court and Congress over the appropriate level of protection afforded to religious liberty under the free exercise guarantee of the First Amendment. This struggle began with the Court's 1990 refusal to protect the sacramental use of peyote under the First Amendment. In doing so, it allowed governmental entities to significantly burden the free exercise of religion. Congress responded by passing the Religious Freedom Restoration Act (RFRA) of 1993, an act that sought to protect the practice of religion from governmental interference. In 1997 the Supreme Court then struck down RFRA in *City of Boerne v. Flores* as an infringement of states' rights and as a violation of the separation of powers doctrine. The Court held that the judiciary, not Congress, possessed the right of judicial review.

In chapter seven, "The Least Dangerous Branch? The Supreme Court's New Judicial Activism," John F. Stack Jr. and Colton C. Campbell explore the revitalization of the Tenth and Eleventh Amendments by the Supreme Court. Led by Chief Justice William Rehnquist and Associate Justices O'Connor, Kennedy, Scalia, and Thomas, the Court is in the process of redefining federal–state relations. This judicial activism in defense of states' rights follows nearly seventy years of federal expansion and prerogative into all corners of American life. The Rehnquist majority has begun to push back congressional assertiveness in the guise of federal power. In a series of major cases the Court has given a boost to state sovereign power at the expense of federal power and privilege.

Finally, in chapter eight, "When Do Courts 'Legislate'? Reflections on Congress and the Court," Nicol C. Rae provides an assessment of the conditions in which the Supreme Court plays a significant legislative role in American politics. He contends that when the Court defies popular public will on major questions of policies, then the branches most responsive to the broader consensus will push the Court to redefine its direction. This is often done through the replacement of justices or the enactment of laws challenging the Court's decisions. For Rae, the Court may on occasion get out in front of issues. This means that the quest for legitimacy and authority by the Supreme Court is determined by institutional constraints (Congress and the presidency) and expressions of popular will.

THE POLITICS OF CONFRONTATION

The relationship between Congress and the Supreme Court is often neglected or mischaracterized. Institutionally, the Court is approached as apolitical, nonpartisan, and removed from politics. Conversely, Congress is portrayed as dominated by special interests and motivated by constituency concerns. Such deeply embedded views, however, distort the relations between these two fundamental institutions of government. As the title of this volume suggests, both branches are engaged in a struggle over policymaking. The contributors underscore that lawmaking is not the sole preserve of Congress nor is the interpretation of laws exclusively the function of the Supreme Court. Lawmaking and law interpreting occur in both branches. Indeed, formalistic distinctions between congressional and judicial functions obscure a complex and fluid process of governing.

As complex institutions, Congress and the Court increasingly confront political and judicial policy matters that demand unorthodox approaches. No longer, for example, may Congress invoke the interstate commerce clause to extend the reach of federal law without compelling justification (*United States v. Lopez* [1995]). Rather, a majority of the Court increasingly insists that federal power give way to the sovereign prerogatives of states. The congressional–judicial balance of power, therefore, is assuming a confrontational tenor where lawmakers see the Supreme Court legislating in many matters rather than simply interpreting the meanings of law, and justices view Congress as progressively eroding traditional boundaries between federal and state power. In the end, each view suggests the importance of the struggle for legitimacy and authority in lawmaking.

We invite the reader to consider the ways in which legislative and judicial functions are heightening the tensions that such convergence creates. We also ask that the reader look critically whenever Congress assumes judicial functions and when the Court, in the words of Justice Black, becomes a superlegislature.

PART ONE

Congressional Objection to Judicial Prerogative

CHAPTER TWO

Congressional Checks on the Judiciary

LOUIS FISHER

Although it is conventional to view the judiciary—and especially the Supreme Court—as the ultimate and final arbiter of constitutional law, numerous examples over two centuries suggest a more dynamic and less hierarchical model. Throughout this period, Congress has disagreed with court decisions and has pressed its own independent views on the meaning of the Constitution, often with substantial effect. Similar challenges have come from presidents, who assert their own right to reach independent and coequal constitutional opinions. In this ebb and flow, all three branches strive for ascendancy without ever attaining it. Repeatedly, the Court has recognized that it is not the only branch with authority and capacity to interpret the Constitution. The result is a judiciary that is regularly checked and guided by the other branches.

THE CLAIM FOR JUDICIAL SUPREMACY

Particularly in the twentieth century, scholars, judges, and sometimes members of Congress claim that the U.S. Supreme Court has the "last word" on the meaning of the Constitution. Under this theory, if Congress disagrees with a Court ruling the only alternative is to pass a constitutional amendment to overturn the Court. This claim of judicial supremacy overlooks much of the flexibility and political considerations that characterize the relationship between the judiciary and other elements of the political system: Congress, the president, the states, and the general public.

Judicial Positions on Finality

Justices of the Supreme Court take different positions regarding the finality of Court decisions. Some see a decision as wholly binding on nonjudicial parties, including Congress. Others leave room for a sharing of jurisdiction among federal institutions over statutory and constitutional questions. Although Justice Robert H. Jackson once said, "We are not final because we are infallible, but we are infallible only because we are final," history demonstrates convincingly that the Court is neither infallible nor final (*Brown v. Allen* 1953, 540). Its decisions are regularly reshaped by other political institutions, both at the national and the state levels. In a speech, Jackson acknowledged the force of politics and majority rule in the shaping of constitutional values:

> [L]et us not deceive ourselves; long-sustained public opinion does influence the process of constitutional interpretation. Each new member of the ever-changing personnel of our courts brings to his task the assumptions and accustomed thought of a later period. The practical play of the forces of politics is such that judicial power has often delayed but never permanently defeated the persistent will of a substantial majority. (Jackson 1953, 761)

To Justice Frankfurter, "the ultimate touchstone of constitutionality is the Constitution itself and not what we have said about it" (*Graves v. New York ex rel. O'Keefe* 1939, 491–92). Before joining the Court, he put the point more bluntly to President Franklin D. Roosevelt, "People have been taught to believe that when the Supreme Court speaks it is not they who speak but the Constitution, whereas, of course, in so many vital cases, it is *they* who speak and not the Constitution" (quoted in Freedman 1967, 383).

Chief Justice Earl Warren cautioned against an overreliance on the courts for the protection of constitutional rights. In an article in 1962 he wrote with regret about *Hirabayashi v. United States* (1943) (*Graves v. New York ex rel. O'Keefe* 1939, 491–92), in which the Court unanimously upheld a curfew order directed against more than 100,000 Japanese Americans, about two-thirds of them naturally born United States citizens. Warren said that the "fact that the Court rules in a case like *Hirabayashi* that a given program is constitutional does not necessarily answer the question whether, in a broader sense, it actually is" (Warren 1962, 193). The Court's failure to invalidate a governmental action did not, by itself, mean that constitutional standards had been followed. Warren emphasized that in a democratic society "it is still the Legislature and the elected Executive who have the primary responsibility for fashioning and executing policy consistent with the Constitution." He even warned against depending too much on Congress and the president, "[T]he day-to-day job of upholding the Constitution really lies elsewhere. It rests, realistically, on the shoulders of every citizen."

At certain points in our constitutional history, there has been a compelling need for an authoritative and binding decision by the Supreme Court. The unanimous ruling in *Cooper v. Aaron* (1958), signed by each justice, was essential in dealing with the Little Rock desegregation crisis. Another unanimous decision in *United States v. Nixon* (1974) disposed of the confrontation between President Nixon and the judiciary regarding the Watergate tapes. For the most part, however, court decisions are tentative and reversible like other political events (Fisher 2001).

The "Binding Precedent" of Marbury

The Supreme Court's 1803 opinion in *Marbury v. Madison* is the most famous case for the proposition that the Court is supreme on constitutional questions. Chief Justice John Marshall stated that it is "emphatically the province and duty of the judicial department to say what the law is" (*Marbury v. Madison*, 177). When this statement is placed in context, both legal and political, there is less sweep to Marshall's words than contemporary authors often imply. Nonetheless, *Marbury* is often cited by the Court as evidence that it alone delivers the "final word" on the meaning of the Constitution. According to the Little Rock decision, *Marbury* "declared the basic principle that the federal judiciary is supreme in the exposition of the law of the Constitution" (*Cooper v. Aaron* 1958, 18). A similar position appears in *Baker v. Carr* (1962, 211), "Deciding whether a matter has in any measure been committed by the Constitution to another branch of government, or whether action of that branch exceeds whatever authority has been committed, is itself a delicate exercise in constitutional interpretation, and a responsibility of this Court as ultimate interpreter of the Constitution." In the *Powell v. McCormack* (1969, 211) decision, the Court referred to itself as the "ultimate interpreter" of the Constitution. It is the ultimate interpreter among federal courts, but state courts operating within state constitutions can reach different (and binding) conclusions about constitutional values.

Moreover, "ultimate interpreter" does not mean exclusive interpreter. The courts expect other branches of government to interpret the Constitution in their initial deliberations. As the Court noted in the Watergate tapes case, "In the performance of assigned constitutional duties each branch of the Government must initially interpret the Constitution, and the interpretation of its powers by any branch is due great respect from the others" (*United States v. Nixon* 1974, 703).

The Scope and Reach of Marbury

No specific language in the Constitution gives the Supreme Court the power to declare unconstitutional an act of Congress or the president. Several delegates at the constitutional convention at Philadelphia spoke in favor of judicial review when invoked against *state* laws. State actions inconsistent with the U.S. Constitution "would clearly not be valid," said Gouverneur Morris, and judges "would consider them as null & void" (quoted in Farrand 1937, vol. 2, 92). Judicial review over Congress and the president, as coequal branches, is much more difficult to establish. Granted, the Court would need power to strike down congressional legislation that threatened the integrity or existence of the judiciary. Such actions of self-defense are part of the system of checks and balances and separation of powers. Beyond those justifications, the picture is quite unclear.

Chief Justice Marshall's decision in *Marbury* represents what many regard as the definitive basis for judicial review over congressional and presidential actions. But Marshall's opinion stands for a much more modest claim. He stated that it is "emphatically the province and duty of the judicial department to say what the law is." So it is, but Congress and the president are also empowered under the Constitution to "say what the law is." Marshall's statement can stand only for the proposition that the Court is responsible for stating what it thinks a statute means, after which Congress may enact another law to override the Court's interpretation. The Court states what the law is on the day the decision comes down; the law may change later. I will cite several examples of this institutional interplay.

In 1803, Marshall did not think he was powerful enough to give orders to Congress and the president. After the election of 1800, with the Jeffersonians in control of government, the Federalist Court was in no position to dictate to the other branches. Marshall realized that he could not uphold the constitutionality of section 13 of the Judiciary Act of 1789 and direct Secretary of State James Madison to deliver the commissions to the disappointed would-be judges. President Thomas Jefferson and Madison would have ignored such an order. Everyone knew that, including Marshall. As Chief Justice Warren Burger noted, "The Court could stand hard blows, but not ridicule, and the ale houses would rock with hilarious laughter" had Marshall issued a mandamus that the Jefferson administration ignored (Burger 1985, 14).

Under these circumstances, it is doubtful that Marshall believed that the Court was supreme on constitutional interpretation. The impeachment hearings of Judge Pickering and Justice Chase underscore this point. *Marbury* was issued on February 24, 1803. The House impeached Pickering on March 2, 1803 and the Senate convicted him on March 12, 1804. As soon as the House impeached Pickering, it turned its guns on Chase. If that move succeeded, Marshall had reason to believe he was next in line.

With these threats pressing upon the Court, Marshall wrote to Chase on January 23, 1805, suggesting that members of Congress did not have to impeach judges because they objected to their judicial opinions. Instead, Congress could simply review and reverse objectionable decisions through the regular legislative process. Here is Marshall's language in a letter to Chase:

I think the modern doctrine of impeachment should yield to an appellate jurisdiction in the legislature. A reversal of those legal opinions deemed unsound by
the legislature would certainly better comport with the mildness of our character
than [would] a removal of the Judge who has rendered them unknowing of his
fault. (quoted in Beveridge 1919, 177)

The meaning of *Marbury* is placed in proper perspective when we recall that
Marshall never again struck down a congressional statute during his long tenure,
which lasted from 1801 to 1835. Instead, he played a consistently supportive
role in upholding congressional power. In the years following *Marbury*, he
upheld the power of Congress to exercise its commerce power, to create a U.S.
bank, and to discharge other constitutional responsibilities, whether express or
implied, without being second-guessed by the Court. The judiciary functioned
as a yea-saying, not a negative, branch.

POLITICAL AND LEGISLATIVE PRESSURES

Other than the checks expressly stated in the Constitution, federal courts are
subject to constraints that arise through the normal functioning of the political
system. These limitations operate not only when courts sustain the constitutionality of a statute but also when they declare it to be invalid.

When the Court Upholds Constitutionality

When the Court decides that a congressional statute or a presidential action
is constitutional, the controversy may remain open for different treatments by
the legislative and executive branches.

The U.S. Bank

In 1832, President Andrew Jackson received a bill to recharter the U.S.
Bank. Several presidents before him and previous congresses had decided that
the bank was constitutional. In *McCulloch v. Maryland* (1819), the Supreme
Court had ruled that the bank was constitutional. Nevertheless, Jackson
vetoed the bill on the ground that it was unconstitutional. In his veto message, he said that he had taken an oath of office to support the Constitution
"as he understands it, and not as it is understood by others." The opinion of
judges, he said,

has no more authority over Congress than the opinion of Congress had over the
judges, and on that point the President is independent of both. The authority of
the Supreme Court must not, therefore, be permitted to control the Congress or
the Executive when acting in their legislative capacities, but to have only such
influence as the force of their reasoning may deserve. (quoted in Richardson
1897, vol. 3, 1145)

All subsequent presidents have followed Jackson's position on the veto power. Regardless of the constitutional decisions reached by Congress and the courts, presidents may independently analyze the constitutionality of bills presented to them.

Independent Counsel

Presidents Reagan and Clinton signed legislation creating and reauthorizing the office of independent counsel. In *Morrison v. Olson* (1988), the Supreme Court upheld the constitutionality of the independent counsel statute. Despite those actions, any future Congress or president retains the independence to decide whether to reauthorize the office of independent counsel. If Congress were to pass such legislation, a president could veto the measure on the ground that it encroaches upon the executive power granted to the president by the Constitution. The holding of the Court in 1988 simply means that Congress and the president are at liberty to create this office if they want to. They may rethink and revisit the statute at any time.

Women's Rights

In *Bradwell v. State* (1873), the Supreme Court held that denying women the right to practice law was not a violation of the Fourteenth Amendment guarantee of privileges and immunities. In 1878, the U.S. House of Representatives passed a bill to remove legal disabilities that prevented women from practicing law. When asked whether the question had ever been brought before the Supreme Court, Representative Roderick R. Butler (R-Tenn.) replied, "It has; and they have decided that as the law now stands women cannot be admitted" (*Congressional Record* 1878, 1235). The bill passed the House by a margin of 169 to 87.

The Senate Judiciary Committee reported the bill adversely, arguing that the Supreme Court and every other federal court are authorized to make their own rules regulating the admission of persons to practice, "so that there is now no obstacle of law whatever to the admission of women to practice in those courts" (*Congressional Record* 1878, 1821). Senator Joseph McDonald (D-Ind.) conceded that the Court might change its rules to permit women to practice before it, "but as it does not seem inclined to do so, I do not think it is wrong for us to prescribe in this case a rule for the Supreme Court" (*Congressional Record* 1879, 1083). Senator George Hoar (R-Mass.) rejected the argument that the Supreme Court should be left alone to decide by its own rules who may practice before it, "Now, with the greatest respect for that tribunal, I conceive that the law-making and not the law-expounding power in this Government ought to determine the question what class of citizens shall be clothed with the office of the advocate" (*Congressional Record* 1879, 1084). The bill passed the Senate, 39 to 20. As enacted into law, the bill provided that any woman "who shall have been a member of the bar of the highest court of any State or Territory or of the Supreme

Court of the District of Columbia for the space of three years, and shall have maintained a good standing before such court, and who shall be a person of good moral character, shall, on motion, and the production of such record, be admitted to practice before the Supreme Court of the United States" (*Statutes at Large*, vol. 20, 292).

Financial Privacy

In 1972, agents from the Treasury Department's Alcohol, Tobacco, and Firearms Bureau presented grand jury subpoenas to two banks in which a suspect maintained accounts. Without advising the depositor that subpoenas had been served, the banks supplied the government with microfilms of checks, deposit slips, and other records. The Supreme Court, in *United States v. Miller* (1976, 438), held that a Fourth Amendment interest could not be vindicated in court by challenging such a subpoena. The Court treated the materials as business records of a bank, not private papers of a person.

Congress responded by passing the Right to Financial Privacy Act of 1978. Representative Charles W. Whalen (R-Ohio) explained that the primary purpose of the statute was to prevent warrantless government searches of bank and credit records that reveal the nature of one's private affairs. The government should not have access "except with the knowledge of the subject individual or else with the supervision of the courts" (*Congressional Record* 1978, 33310). Representative John H. Rousselot (R-Calif.) remarked about the responsibility of Congress to redress the shortcomings of the Court's decision. In essence, certain safeguards to Fourth Amendment rights that were unavailable because of the Supreme Court's decision were now secured by congressional action.

Recess Appointments

Another example of independent legislative and executive analysis comes from the field of recess appointments. The president's constitutional authority to make recess appointments to the federal courts was upheld by the Second Circuit in 1962 and the Ninth Circuit in 1985 (*United States v. Allocco* 1962; *United States v. Woodley* 1985). Although this practice was upheld in the courts, Congress had expressed opposition to these appointments. In 1960, the Senate adopted a resolution objecting to recess appointments to the courts, and the House Judiciary Committee conducted a study of this type of appointment. Both Houses pointed to serious constitutional issues: circumvention of the Senate's role in confirming regular appointments; judges serving in a recess capacity without the independence of a lifetime appointment; and litigants forced to argue their case before a part-time federal judge (Fisher 1997, 43–45). Because of opposition to this practice, no president since Eisenhower has used the recess appointment power to place someone on the Supreme Court, and no president since Carter has used the power to place someone on the lower courts.

Similar to the independent counsel issue, the courts have told the political branches that they may place recess appointees on the federal courts if they want to, but if the branches have constitutional doubts about the practice they can rely on the regular confirmation process for lifetime appointments. The political branches have chosen to do the latter.

Religious Freedom

In *Goldman v. Weinberger* (1986), the Supreme Court decided a case involving Captain Simcha Goldman, who was told by the Air Force that he could not wear his yarmulke indoors while on duty. The Court upheld the constitutionality of the Air Force regulation, reasoning that the regulation was necessary for military discipline, unity, and order. In effect, Air Force needs outweighed Goldman's free exercise of religion. Within a year, Congress attached to a military authorization bill language permitting military personnel to wear conservative, unobtrusive religious apparel indoors, provided that it does not interfere with their military duties (*Statutes at Large,* vol. 101, sec. 508, 1086–87). The debate in the House and the Senate demonstrated that members of Congress were capable of analyzing constitutional rights and giving greater protection to individuals than was available from the Supreme Court.

When the Court Finds Unconstitutionality

If the Court decides that a governmental action is unconstitutional, it is usually more difficult for Congress and the president to contest the judiciary. Congress frequently rewrites legislation to redress deficiencies found by the courts. But even in this category there are examples of effective legislative and executive actions in response to court rulings.

Slavery

In his inaugural address in 1857, President James Buchanan announced that the dispute over slavery in the territories "is a judicial question, which legitimately belongs to the Supreme Court of the United States, before whom it is now pending, and will, it is understood, be speedily and finally settled. To their decision, in common with all good citizens, I shall cheerfully submit, whatever this may be." Two days later Chief Justice Taney handed down *Dred Scott,* holding that Congress could not prohibit slavery in the territories and that blacks were not U.S. citizens (*Dred Scott v. Sandford* 1857, 393).

Far from settling the matter and providing the "final word" on the slavery issue, the Court's decision split the country. During the debates of 1858, Senator Stephen A. Douglas (D-Ill.) supported *Dred Scott* while his opponent, Abraham Lincoln, accepted the decision only as it affected the particular litigants. However, he rejected the larger policy questions decided by the Court, including the issues of slavery in the territories and citizenship of blacks. He considered those parts of the decision nullities, to be left to political resolution outside the courts (Basler 1953, vol. 2, 516).

Lincoln regarded the Court as a coequal, not a superior, branch of government. In his inaugural address in 1861, he denied that solely the Court could settle constitutional questions. If government policy on "vital questions affecting the whole people is to be irrevocably fixed" by the Court, "the people will have ceased to be their own rulers, having to that extent practically resigned their Government into the hands of that eminent tribunal" (Richardson 1897, vol. 7, 3210).

Dred Scott was eventually overturned by the Thirteenth, Fourteenth, and Fifteenth Amendments, but before those amendments were ratified, Congress and the president had already taken steps to repudiate the main tenets of the decision. Congress passed legislation in 1862 to prohibit slavery in the territories (*Statutes at Large,* vol. 12, 432). Also in 1862, Attorney General Bates released a long opinion in which he held that neither color nor race could deny American blacks the right of citizenship. With regard to *Dred Scott,* he said that the case "as it stands of record, does not determine, nor purport to determine" the question of blacks to be citizens. What Chief Justice Taney said about citizenship was pure dicta and "of no authority as a judicial decision." Bates concluded, "[T]he *free man of color,* . . . if born in the United States, is a citizen of the United States" (10 Op. Att'y Gen. 382 1862, 413).

Child Labor Legislation

In passing the first child labor law in 1916, Congress relied on the commerce power. The Supreme Court in *Hammer v. Dagenhart* (1918) held that statute to be unconstitutional. The following year Congress passed legislation again to regulate child labor, this time relying on its power to tax. In *Bailey v. Drexel Furniture Co.* (1922) the Court struck down the second child labor law as well. At that point Congress passed a constitutional amendment in 1924 to give it the power to regulate child labor. By 1937, only twenty-eight of the necessary thirty-six states had ratified the amendment, and there was little hope of securing the additional states. After a major collision between the Court and the political branches throughout the 1930s, Congress returned to the commerce power when it included a child labor provision in the Fair Labor Standards Act of 1938. The issue was taken to the Supreme Court, which in *United States v. Darby* (1941) unanimously upheld the child labor section.

This record—from 1916 to 1941—marked an exceptionally lengthy dialogue between Congress and the Court, with the legislative branch eventually prevailing. The Court later admitted in *Prudential Ins. Co. v. Benjamin* (1946, 415) that "the history of judicial limitation of congressional power over commerce, when exercised affirmatively, has been more largely one of retreat than of ultimate victory."

Sedition

In *Pennsylvania v. Nelson* (1956, 504), the Supreme Court invalidated a state sedition law because the Smith Act, passed by Congress, regulated the same subject. The Court concluded that it had been the intent of Congress to occupy the whole field of sedition. The author of the Smith Act, Representative Howard W. Smith (D-Va.), immediately denied that he had ever intended the result reached by the Court. In fact, even before the Court decided the question, he criticized the holding of the Supreme Court of Pennsylvania that the Smith Act preempted state efforts to regulate sedition (*Congressional Record* 1955, 142–43). He introduced a bill to prohibit the courts from construing a congressional statute "as indicating an intent on the part of Congress to occupy a field in which such act operates, to the exclusion of all State laws on the same subject matter, unless such act contains an express provision to that effect" (*Congressional Record* 1955, 142).

Congressional committees reported legislation to permit concurrent jurisdiction by the federal government and the states in the areas of sedition and subversion. Smith explained that the purpose of his bill was to say to the Supreme Court, "Do not undertake to read the minds of the Congress; we, in the Congress, think ourselves more capable of knowing our minds than the Supreme Court. . . . We are telling you that when we get ready to repeal a State law or preempt a field, we will say so and we will not leave it to the Supreme Court to guess whether we are or not" (*Congressional Record* 1958, 14139–40). His bill passed the House of Representatives by the vote of 241 to 155 (*Congressional Record* 1958, 14162). The measure was never taken up on the Senate floor.

In 1959, these bills were again under consideration. Shortly before the legislation was debated by the House, the Court in *Uphaus v. Wyman* (1959) "distinguished" its 1956 decision and held that a state could investigate subversive activities against itself. To this extent state and federal sedition laws could coexist. The Court's modification satisfied congressional critics, who thought the preemption doctrine announced in 1956 intruded upon state sovereignty, and put an end to the confrontation between the judicial and congressional branches.

Congressional Investigations

In 1970, the House Committee on Internal Security prepared a report on "Limited Survey of Honoraria Given Guest Speakers for Engagements at Colleges and Universities." The study included the names of leftist or antiwar speakers and the amounts they received. The ACLU obtained a copy of the galleys and asked for an injunction. In *Hentoff v. Ichord* (1970, 1183), District Judge Gesell ruled that the report served no legislative purpose and was issued solely for the sake of exposure or intimidation. He ordered the Public Printer and the Superintendent of Documents not to print the report "or any portion, restatement or facsimile thereof," with the possible exception of placing the report in the *Congressional Record*. Gesell claimed that "the authority of a congressional committee to publish and distribute a report at public expense is not unlimited but is subject to judicial review in the light of the circumstances presented" (*Hentoff v. Ichord* 1970, 1181).

On December 14, 1970, the House of Representatives passed a resolution that told the courts, in essence, to step back. During the course of the debate, members of Congress explained that it was not the practice of the House to print committee reports in the *Congressional Record*. Moreover, Judge Gesell's order "runs afoul not only of the speech and debate clause—Article I, section 6—of the Constitution, but obstructs the execution of other constitutional commitments of the House as well, including Article I, section 5, which authorizes each House to determine the rules of its proceedings, and requires each House to publish its proceedings" (*Congressional Record* 1970, 41358).

The resolution stated that the new committee report was a "restatement" of the previous one and ordered the Public Printer and the Superintendent of Documents to print and distribute it. With an eye toward Judge Gesell and others who might stand in the way, the resolution provided that all persons "are further advised, ordered, and enjoined to refrain from molesting, intimidating, damaging, arresting, imprisoning, or punishing any person because of his participation in" publishing the report (*Congressional Record* 1970, 18). The resolution passed by a large bipartisan margin of 302 to 54 and the report was printed without any further interference from the judiciary (*Congressional Record* 1970, 41373).

Legislative Vetoes

The collision between Congress and the judiciary in 1970 was unusually abrupt. For the most part, the legislative–executive dialogue is more nuanced and subtle. In *Immigration and Naturalization Service v. Chadha* (1983), the Supreme Court struck down the "legislative veto" as unconstitutional. Congress no longer attempts to use one-House or two-House vetoes to control the executive branch, but it continues to use committee and subcommittee votes to monitor agency action. Some five hundred of these vetoes—most of them placed in appropriations bills—have been enacted since *Chadha*. No one has challenged these vetoes in court and no one is likely to.

Judicial Invitations

During the 1930s and 1940s, after Congress and the Court had clashed on a tax issue, the Supreme Court invited Congress to pass legislation and challenge previous rulings. As it noted in *Helvering v. Griffiths* (1943, 400–401), "There is no reason to doubt that this Court may fall into error as may other branches of the Government. Nothing in the history or attitude of this Court should give rise to legislative embarrassment if in the performance of its duty a legislative body feels impelled to enact laws which may require the Court to reexamine its previous judgment or doctrine." The Court explained that it is less able than other branches "to extricate itself from error," because it can reconsider a matter "only when it is again properly brought before it as a case or controversy" (*Helvering v. Griffiths* 1943, 401). By overruling itself, the Court admits its ability on an earlier occasion to commit error. "Congress and the courts," said Justice Stone in his dissenting opinion in *United States v. Butler* (1936, 87), "both unhappily may falter or be mistaken in the performance of their constitutional duty."

Commerce Clause

In *Leisy v. Hardin* (1890), the Supreme Court ruled that a state's prohibition of intoxicating liquors could not be applied to "original packages" or kegs. Only after the original package was broken into smaller packages could the state exercise control. The Court qualified its opinion by saying that the states could not exclude incoming articles "without congressional permission" (*Leisy v. Hardin* 1890, 125). Within a matter of months, Congress considered legislation to overturn the decision. During debate, Senator George Edmunds (R-Vt.) said that the opinions of the Supreme Court regarding Congress "are of no more value to us than ours are to it. We are just as independent of the Supreme Court of the United States as it is of us, and every judge will admit it." If members of Congress concluded that the Court had made an error "are we to stop and say that is the end of the law and the mission of civilization in the United States for that reason? I take it not" (*Congressional Record* 1890, 4964).

Congress quickly overturned the Court's decision by passing legislation that made intoxicating liquors, upon their arrival in a state or territory, subject to the police powers "to the same extent and in the same manner as though such liquids or liquors had been produced in such State or Territory, and shall not be exempt therefrom by reason of being introduced therein in original packages or otherwise" (*Statutes at Large*, vol. 26, 313). A year later, in *In re Rahrer,* the Court upheld the constitutionality of this statute.

Criminal Procedures

Jencks v. United States (1957) involved access by defendants to government files bearing on their trial. On the basis of statements by two informants for the FBI, the government prosecuted Clinton Jencks for failing to state that he was a member of the Communist Party. He asked that the FBI reports be turned over to the trial judge for examination to determine whether they had value in impeaching the statements of the two informants. The Supreme Court went beyond Jencks's request by ordering the government to produce for Jencks's inspection all FBI reports "touching the events and activities" at issue in the trial. The Court specifically rejected the option of producing government documents to the trial judge for his determination of relevance and materiality.

In their concurrence, Justices Burton and Harlan believed that Jencks was only entitled to have the records submitted to the trial judge. A dissent by Justice Clark, agreeing that the documents should be delivered only to the trial judge, encouraged Congress to act, "Unless the Congress changes the rule announced by the Court today, those intelligence agencies of our Government engaged in law enforcement may as well close up shop, for the Court has opened their files to the criminal and thus afforded him a Roman holiday for rummaging through confidential information as well as vital national secrets" (*Jencks v. United States* 1957, 668).

The Court announced its decision on June 3, 1957. Both the House and the Senate quickly held hearings and reported remedial legislation. The Jencks Bill passed the Senate by voice vote on August 26 and passed the House on August 27 by a vote of 351 to 17. The conference report was adopted with huge majorities: 74 to 2 in the Senate and 315 to 0 in the House. The bill became law on September 2, 1957. The statute provides that in any federal criminal prosecution, no statement or report in the possession of the government "which was made by a Government witness or prospective Government witness (other than the defendant) to an agent of the Government shall be the subject of subpoena, discovery, or inspection unless said witness has testified on direct examination in the trial of the case." If a witness testifies, statements may be delivered to the defendant for examination and use unless the United States claims that the statement contains irrelevant matter, in which case the court shall inspect the statement in camera. The judge may excise irrelevant portions of the statement before submitting it to the defendant (*Statutes at Large,* vol. 71, 595).

Search and Seizure

In *Zurcher v. Stanford Daily* (1978), the Supreme Court ruled that law enforcement officials could obtain a warrant and enter the premises of a newspaper to conduct a search for evidence regarding another party. The Court's approval of third-party searches and the threat to a free press triggered nationwide protests and congressional hearings. The Court, in fact, had invited Congress to act if it considered the Court's decision too restrictive on free press rights. The Court stated that nothing in the Fourth Amendment prevented legislative or executive efforts to establish "nonconstitutional protections against possible abuses of the search warrant procedure" (*Zurcher v. Stanford Daily* 1978, 567).

Apparently the word "nonconstitutional" was an effort to permit the participation of Congress and the president without jeopardizing the Court's supposed monopoly on constitutional questions. Yet Congress had to do precisely what the Court had done: balance the interests of law enforcement against free press. Legislation in 1980 limited newsroom searches by requiring, with certain exceptions, a subpoena instead of the more intrusive warrant (*Statutes at Large,* vol. 94, 1879). If a newspaper or anyone with a First Amendment interest is required by subpoena to respond, they surrender only the requested document. Law enforcement officials do not enter their space to begin a general search through files, wastepaper baskets, and other sources.

The Role of Custom

Congressional and executive practices over a number of years have been instrumental in fixing the meaning of the Constitution. In *Stuart v. Laird* (1803, 309), faced with a challenge to constitutionality of the Judiciary Act of 1789, the Supreme Court stated that "practice, and acquiescence under it, for a number of years, commencing with the organization of the judicial system, affords an irresistible answer, and has indeed fixed the construction. It is a contemporary interpretation of the most forcible nature." In upholding the president's power to remove executive officials, the Court in 1903 based its ruling largely on the "universal practice of the government for over a century" (*Shurtleff v. United States*, 1903, 316).

Presidential action acquiesced in by Congress can become a justification for the exercise of power. Presidential decisions in withdrawing public lands from private use can, over a period of years, "clearly indicate that the long-continued practice, known to and acquiesced in by Congress, would raise a presumption that the withdrawals had been made in pursuance of its consent or of a recognized administrative power of the Executive in the management of the public lands" (*United States v. Midwest Oil Co.* 1915, 474). The cumulative force of these customs has helped to transform the Constitution over time.

In the Steel Seizure Case of 1952, challenging the seizure of steel mills by President Truman during the Korean War, several justices spoke about the force of custom in shaping constitutional law. Justice Jackson spoke about a "zone of twilight" in which Congress has neither granted nor denied authority, allowing substantial discretion for presidential power. He remarked, "congressional inertia, indifference or quiescence may sometimes, as a practical matter, enable, if not invite, measures on independent presidential responsibility. In this area, any actual test of power is likely to depend on the imperatives of events and contemporary imponderables rather than on abstract theories of law" (*Youngstown Co. v. Sawyer* 1952, 635–37).

In other words, the constitutionality of an action is sometimes determined not by analyzing the words or intent of the Constitution but rather the political context in which a president acts. Other statements have tempered Jackson's analysis. Justice Frankfurter earlier noted, "Illegality cannot attain legitimacy through practice" (*Inland Waterways Corp. v. Young* 1940, 524), and Professor Gerhard Casper has written that "unconstitutional practices cannot become legitimate by the mere lapse of time" (Casper 1976, 479; see Glennon 1984).

CONCLUSION

Justice Frankfurter put the Court's work in perspective by reminding his readers that it is "important to bear in mind that this Court can only hope to set the limits and point the way. It falls to the lot of legislative bodies and administrative officials to find practical solutions within the frame of our decisions" (*Niemotko v. Maryland* 1951, 275–76). At times the legislative and executive branches work within the broad contours of a judicial decision. On other occasions it is the judiciary that seeks practical solutions within the frame of congressional statutes and executive precedents.

A belief in judicial supremacy imposes a burden that the Court cannot carry. It is not strong enough—constitutionally, institutionally, and politically—to dictate to other branches and to the public. Its destiny is more modest, calling for a wise mix of leadership and prudence. Constitutional law develops by a combination of judicial rulings, statutes, executive action, political accommodations, and custom. Through these pressures and realities, institutions outside the courts play a decisive role in shaping not only constitutional values but also constitutional doctrines. The Court functions best when it operates within these boundaries.

There is no reason for Congress to defer automatically to the judiciary because of its supposed technical skills and political independence. Much of constitutional law depends on fact-finding and the balancing of competing values, areas in which Congress can justifiably claim substantial expertise. Each decision by a court is subject to scrutiny by private citizens and public officials. What is "final" at one stage of our political development may be reopened at some later date, leading to revisions, fresh interpretations, and reversals of Supreme Court doctrines. Members of Congress have both the authority and the capability to participate constructively in constitutional interpretation.

Through this process of interaction among the branches, all three institutions are able to expose weaknesses, hold excesses in check, and gradually forge a consensus on constitutional values. Also through this process, the public has an opportunity to add legitimacy and a meaning to what might otherwise be an alien and short-lived document.

CHAPTER THREE

Separation of Powers and Judicial Impeachment

MARY L. VOLCANSEK

The ability of the U.S. House of Representatives to impeach and the Senate to try and possibly convict federal judges is one element of separation of powers. The tripartite division of American government is usually conceived as a three-player game, involving Congress, the Supreme Court, and the president, each armed with "checks" to "balance" the others. The place of the much larger federal judiciary in this enterprise is largely neglected, and interest is focused solely on the highest court. District and appellate court judges draw attention as mere pawns in a strategic game between the president and the Senate when nominations reach the confirmation stage. Subsequent checks on federal judges through impeachment or the threat of it are typically mentioned, if at all, only in passing. Moreover, impeachment is portrayed as an exclusively legislative issue, and any executive part in the process is disregarded. In this chapter I offer a model of the judicial impeachment process that presents it as a game, one involving the legislative, executive, and entire judicial branches of the national government, and illustrate the model with historical examples. I also argue that this conceptual shift enables consideration of the U.S. system in a larger, cross-national context.

Political leaders delegate to courts the power to resolve disputes and apply the rules (Stone Sweet 2000), since courts are necessary to enforce the deals the rulers negotiate among themselves and with interest groups. Courts cannot, however, always be counted on to act in the best interests of the delegating body. Thus, judicial independence becomes a sticking point, since the greater the autonomy of the judges, the greater the potential for their unreliability (Landes and Posner 1975). Judicial independence is usually secured through the twin principles of security of tenure and salary, but the U.S. system at least, can be penetrated by impeachment or even by threats of impeachment. Thus, judges must anticipate the consequences of their decisions, just as the legislative and executive branches try to predict how judges will respond to their mandates. Impeachment of judges is generally regarded as a rather useless device, since the unwritten rule seems to be hands-off-the-courts, "unless a judge is insane, incompetent or crooked" (quoted in Ramseyer 1994, 725). Even if that conventional wisdom holds true, the mere threat of potential impeachment may deflect a judge from a particular decision that might signal an unacceptable level of judicial unreliability.

SEPARATION OF POWERS MODEL

Courts are typically viewed as exogenous factors in the policymaking process (Scharpf 1997), as mere external veto points (Weaver and Rockman 1993). Such conceptualizations implicitly accept that courts follow the legal model, seeking primarily legal accuracy and legal clarity without regard for policy (Baum 1997). Focus is usually on the highest court and assumes that judicial review is the means by which courts intervene in the policy process. Those notions reinforce the erroneous perceptions that courts are "above" the policymaking process and have the last word (Blondel 1995). Both the attitudinal model that emphasizes the importance of judicial values and ideology (Segal and Spaeth 1993) and the strategic choice model, which adds judicial calculations of feasibility into the equation (Epstein and Knight 1998), argue that judges do more than simply seek legal accuracy and legal clarity in their decision making. Courts possess a potent tool to affect policies through statutory interpretation (Eskridge 1991) and need not rely on the rather blunt instrument of judicial review of legislation to impact the policymaking process. Judicial review is also usually viewed as the primary means by which judges mold policy, but it is used sparingly to invalidate laws in the United States It was used only some 151 or 152 times through 1997 (Abraham 1998). It poses little threat for judicial defection from the bargains struck in Congress or with the executive. Interpretations and application of law are much more likely to be the instruments in the hands of the judges that derail policy goals of the other branches.

Barry Weingast (1996) recognized the significance of courts in the area of statutory interpretation and proposed viewing the policy process as a single continuum involving executive, legislative, and judicial preferences. Even so, in his view, a court can only effectively move a policy closer to its ideal point than to the one agreed upon by the legislative and executive branches if the executive is "indifferent" to a particular policy.

In Weingast's model, illustrated in figure 3.1, L, E, and C are the ideal policy points for the Legislature, Executive, and Court respectively. X represents the point of policy agreement between Congress and the president. Y, a point closer

Figure 3.1   The Court's Role in Separation of Powers Game

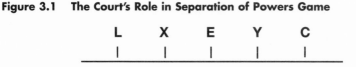

Source: Adapted from B. R. Weingast, "Political Institutions: Rational Choice Perspectives," in A New Handbook of Political Science, R. E. Goodin and H. D. Klingeman, eds. (Oxford: Oxford University Press, 1996), 172–74.

to the ideal point of the Court, is feasible only if the executive is indifferent to the policy (Weingast 1996). The relationship between judicial discretion is, in other words, inverse to the probability of legislative or executive action to overturn statutory interpretations (Hix 1999). Even when the Supreme Court invalidates legislation on constitutional grounds, Congress is not inclined to attempt to overturn the decisions (Ignagni and Meernik 1994). Congressional disinclination further buttresses judicial discretion because of the improbability of congressional override. Perhaps that is why some evidence suggests that justices of the Supreme Court ignore congressional preferences or at least vote their own value preferences despite what lawmakers may prefer (Segal 1997).

Weingast's model of separation of powers fails, however, to take into account the full range of legislative and executive expectations for judicial decisions and is limited to inclusion of the Supreme Court. I propose that the separation of powers game can be better understood through an expanded conception of the goals of each power. Judges at all levels can fail to ratify legislative–executive bargains, not only through judicial review and statutory interpretation, but also through decisions in individual cases that affect policy implementation, policy application, and executive enforcement of policy. Indeed, the U.S. system of decentralized judicial review permits judges at all levels to exercise judicial review, even though the instances of a lower court's invalidating congressional action are rare (Abraham 1998). Lower court judges can, nonetheless, thwart implementation of legislative and executive policy through decisions in criminal law and application or interpretation of all laws.

Congress's goals for the Court are that legislative policies will be faithfully applied or the bargains enforced without judicial discretion or partisanship that is not in line with the ideological leanings that underpin any specific law. Congress also maintains an interest in preserving regime legitimacy that is jeopardized if a judge or judges violate the maxim of impartiality, whether that be for corrupt or other motives. The executive branch shares with the legislative the goal of maintaining regime legitimacy, but also seeks to enforce the law and implement its policy goals through litigation. Judges whose exercise of independence blocks achievement of either legislative or executive goals are potentially subject to censure. The respective institutional goals for each institution are listed in figure 3.2.

Figure 3.2   Institutional Goals for the Judiciary

Congressional Goals		Executive Goals		Judicial Goals
Legislation Faithfully Applied	→	Law Enforced	→	Achieve Legal Clarity and Accuracy
No Partisan Discretion	→	Litigation to Achieve Policy Goals	→	Achieve Policy Preferences
Regime Legitimacy	→	Regime Legitimacy	→	Regime Legitimacy

Impeachment, or its now milder version of complaints filed through the Judicial Disability and Misconduct Act of 1980, is the only formally recognized means by which Congress or the president may insure that judges will faithfully apply legislative–executive bargains. But they are realistically not the only checks available. Impeachment per se is reserved for Congress, with the House of Representatives bringing charges and the Senate acting as trier of fact. In actuality, the executive branch can, through its role of seeing that the law is faithfully executed, prosecute judges whom it views as threats to its goals. It can, thereby, either force the resignation of the errant judge or set an impeachment agenda for Congress. The executive branch can, likewise, through its investigatory arm present Congress with a case for impeachment without resort to criminal proceedings. Threats of impeachment or press leaks of embarrassing information about a judge's alleged conduct can serve as the incentive for the judge's retirement or curtailment of the offending behavior. In other words, the policymaking and policy executing games are not ones in which the courts have the last say and in which the only recourse of the legislature is to impeach, to rewrite legislation, or to propose constitutional amendments to overturn undesirable judicial pronouncements. The executive branch can join as a player in attempts to curb judges who are too independent and thereby too unreliable.

The policymaking game can be transformed, in other words, into one of separation of powers, where all three branches are players and where both Congress and the president can attempt to curtail judicial behavior that interferes with implementation of legislative–executive bargains. Weingast's model of the policy process should, then, be elaborated, first, by recognizing a dynamic quality in which feedback on actions of each branch is received and used in formulating future actions. Second, the entire federal judiciary and not just the Supreme Court should be seen as a player. To illustrate how this has occurred, I will briefly review the thirteen cases of impeachment that have taken place in the United States and explore other cases where the threat of impeachment or other sanctions were used to rein in federal judges.

CONGRESS AND EXECUTIVE ALLIED: PICKERING AND CHASE

Early in the history of the Republic, Jeffersonian Democrats in Congress and in the executive branch allied to curb a Federalist-dominated national judiciary. The election of 1800 brought domination for the first time of both the executive and legislative powers by the Democrats, but the judiciary was completely controlled by the recently ousted Federalists. The newly elected Jeffersonians were anxious to add some of their adherents to the federal bench, but could only do so if a vacancy occurred. Alcoholic and mentally incompetent Federalist Judge John Pickering of New Hampshire presented the Jeffersonians with that opportunity when, in 1803, he rather blatantly ruled on behalf of a fellow Federalist in the case of the ship *Eliza*. Jefferson sent the House of Representatives a summary of Pickering's failings as a judge, and on December 30, 1803 the House voted 45 to 8 to impeach (Bushnell 1992). Jefferson's complicity in and approval of the action is generally agreed upon, and the vote for Pickering's impeachment and subsequent conviction in 1804 was strictly along party lines (Rehnquist 1992). The overt partisanship that characterized the Pickering case has made it peripheral as a precedent for any future cases (Gerhardt 1996). Even so, the concerted effort by the executive and legislative branches was successful in the first use of impeachment to alter the partisan and ideological complexion of the federal bench.

Buoyed by that victory, Jeffersonian Democrats in the House quickly set their sights on another, more powerful target: U.S. Supreme Court Justice Samuel Chase. Jefferson's involvement in the Chase impeachment process can only be inferred and is based on a letter he wrote to Representative Joseph Hopper Nicholson (R-Md.). In that letter, President Jefferson noted "the extraordinary charge of Chace [*sic*] to the Grand Jury at Baltimore," referring to a partisan harangue that Chase had delivered against the extension of the franchise. Jefferson then added, "Ought this seditious and official attack on the principles of our Constitution . . . go unpunished?" (quoted in Baker 1974, 418). Some see that letter as evidence of Jefferson's support for congressional action against Chase (Rehnquist 1992), but others find no evidence that Jefferson was behind the impeachment effort (Smith 1996). Jefferson's party leaders in the House impeached Chase, with or without Jefferson's approval, in 1804, and a trial on eight articles that included Chase's conduct of two Alien and Sedition Act trials and his handling of grand juries took place in 1805. The result for Chase was, however, the opposite of the result for Pickering. Because of the requirement of a two-thirds majority to convict in the Senate, Chase was acquitted on all articles. A majority vote for guilt was forthcoming on three articles, and those split largely on party lines (Bushnell 1992). Even so, a number of Democratic senators broke ranks on the Chase vote, leading to the conclusion that the impeachment began as a partisan endeavor, but was diffused (Gerhardt 1996).

Attacks on the Federalist judiciary continued, and six other federal judges were targeted for congressional investigations. These investigations were clearly motivated by partisanship and were accompanied by the introduction of no fewer than nine judicial removal amendments in Congress. Notably, none of the judges investigated during this period resigned or were removed, and none of the attempts to limit the life-tenure of federal judges succeeded (Van Tassel 1993). Though similar attacks were launched against the judiciary as a whole in the 1830s and 1870s, a concerted presidential–congressional alliance was not witnessed subsequently.

CONGRESSIONAL ASSAULTS

After the impeachment trial of President Andrew Johnson in 1868, Congress emerged as the clearly ascendant institution of the national government. With the exception of Theodore Roosevelt, most presidents were, until 1932, weak in comparison to the legislature. Not surprisingly, therefore, Congress acted alone and successfully to purge the federal judiciary of incumbents who were found wanting, whether for ethical improprieties or as partisan pawns. Between 1903 and 1936, five judges were impeached and another eight were investigated by Congress; four of those investigated resigned (Ten Broek 1939). Indeed, some twenty federal judges have resigned over the years when allegations of misconduct were raised (Van Tassel 1993). Partisanship appears again to have been the over-riding, though not the only, motivation. All but one of those investigated through 1936 were Republicans or Republican appointees, who incurred the ire of a Democratic majority in Congress.

The first impeachment of the twentieth century was that of U.S. District Judge Charles Swayne. The allegations against Swayne reached the House of Representatives from a rather curious source, one that underscored their partisan bias. The Florida legislature passed a resolution asking the House to impeach Swayne as a result of his decisions against the Democratic Party in state election fraud cases. The ensuing investigation by the House culminated with articles of impeachment, none of which addressed the election fraud cases. Interestingly, representatives voted overwhelmingly once to impeach Swayne, but voted a second time on the same articles one month later; in the second tally, the votes followed strict party lines (Bushnell 1992). The Senate trial in 1905 failed to convict, largely because the Republican Party held a majority in the chamber (Bushnell 1992, 213).

Partisanship did not play a role in the 1912 impeachment and 1913 conviction of Robert W. Archbald, a judge of the U.S. Commerce Court who was found to have played a role in a number of elaborate influence-peddling schemes

(Bushnell 1992, 237). The same bipartisan votes did not, however, characterize congressional consideration of allegations against U.S. District Judge Harold Louderback, who was impeached in 1933 and convicted later the same year. In Louderback's case, the San Francisco Bar Association communicated its concerns about Louderback's selection of incompetent receivers in bankruptcy cases, but the majority of the House committee that investigated the charges concluded that censure, not impeachment, was appropriate. Representatives as a whole, however, disregarded that recommendation and passed articles of impeachment. The partisan alignment was not what might have been predicted. Louderback was a Republican, but Republicans seemed more intent on charging him than did the majority Democrats. He was found not guilty in the Senate, where again proportionately more Republicans than might have been anticipated judged him guilty (Bushnell 1992, 263).

The final instance of impeachment in this period was the case of Republican U.S. District Judge Halsted Ritter of south Florida. By the time of his impeachment in 1936, the Democrats had solidified their control of both houses of Congress, and though the allegations against Ritter dated from some six years earlier, he was impeached by the House largely along partisan lines (Bushnell 1992, 272). In the Senate, he was found not guilty on all articles alleging specific acts of misconduct, but then convicted on an omnibus article. Though both Democrats and Republicans in the Senate voted not guilty on all articles, the overwhelming Democratic majority secured conviction on one (Bushnell 1992, 283).

Congress demonstrated that it was capable, with or without the concurrence of the executive, of removing federal judges whom it found undesirable. Even so, partisan motivations were not transparent in the cases of Swayne and Louderback, since the Democrats in the Senate clearly had the requisite votes to convict and remove, but did not. Ideological overtones were typically clear in decisions of the House to pass articles of impeachment and to push cases to a final conclusion. That determination on the part of Democrats in the House often achieved the desired result, even without the acquiescence of the Senate. George English resigned in 1926 after being impeached but prior to a Senate trial. He had, however, been appointed by Woodrow Wilson and was presumably a Democrat. The tactic of simply commencing an investigation in the House against a judge was usually more successful than taking cases to trial before the Senate. During this same period of time, another seven judges, six of whom were Republicans, resigned when investigations began (Ten Broek 1939).

EXECUTIVE ACTIONS

Michael Gerhardt (1996) correctly notes that following the impeachment of Judge Halsted Ritter in 1936, all subsequent judicial impeachments had their origins in the executive branch and allowed the executive to impinge on judicial tenure, albeit indirectly, via the vehicle of criminal prosecutions. The basic logic is that the executive branch can initiate a criminal investigation of a judge with the expectation that he or she will resign. Indeed, that is exactly what did happen with Judge Albert Johnson in 1945, Judge Edwin Thomas in 1937, and Judge Herbert Fogel in 1978 (Van Tassel 1993). Should a resignation not, however, be forthcoming, the Justice Department can take the case to trial and seek a conviction. This strategy was successful in removing Judges Martin Manton in 1939 and Otto Kerner in 1974, and neither judge resigned until after conviction (Volcansek 1993).

Even criminal convictions no longer assure, however, that the targeted judge will relinquish the bench. Judges Harry Claiborne, Walter Nixon, Robert Aguilar, and Robert Collins were all convicted in the 1980s, although Aguilar's conviction was ultimately overturned on appeal. None resigned, and Collins was in prison, but still technically a sitting U.S. district judge in 1993 (Gerhardt 1996). Both Harry Claiborne and Walter Nixon were eventually removed from their judicial offices, but only through the two-chamber impeachment process. The prosecutions of both, as well as that of Aguilar, were flawed; or, as Senator Terry Sanford said of the Walter Nixon case, "it is more than regrettable that the Justice Department made a criminal of this judge" (quoted in Volcansek 1993, 150). More important, in the cases of Judges Claiborne and Nixon, the fact of prior criminal conviction pre-determined the result of any congressional action. Were the judges not removed, convicted felons would be occupying seats on the federal bench (Volcansek 1993).

The saga of Alcee L. Hastings is among the more bizarre in the annals of American politics. District Court Judge Hastings was tried for bribery and solicitation of bribes, but acquitted by a trial jury. He was nonetheless impeached in the House of Representatives and convicted in the Senate in 1989 (Volcansek 1993). In 1993, he took his seat in the House of Representatives, as a duly elected Democratic member of Congress from south Florida's 23rd District, a seat he still holds (Gerhardt 1996).

MOTIVES FOR REMOVALS

The fact that a judge was removed from office does not necessarily mean that he had committed high crimes and misdemeanors or that he was a victim of political vendettas. The problem of sorting out the motives behind the instigation of removal mechanisms, whether they commenced in Congress, the executive, or both, requires some inferential reasoning. A total of twenty judges have resigned in the face of allegations of misbehavior, and thirteen judges have been impeached by the House of Representatives (Van Tassel 1993). West Humphreys was, for example, impeached and removed in 1862 for loyalty to the

Confederacy. Some fifteen other federal judges resigned for that reason, but when Humphreys did not, there seemed to be little choice but for Congress to use its impeachment and trial procedure (Van Tassel 1993). Similarly, four judges during the Grant administration resigned when congressional investigations focused on them, but some rather clear evidence of a climate of corruption at that time exists.

Overtly partisan motives were apparent when the Jeffersonian Democrats attempted to remove Federalist judges John Pickering and Samuel Chase. Particularly since Jeffersonians dominated the executive branch and both chambers of Congress, the tantalizing question is how Chase escaped removal. The explanations likely lie in a combination of circumstances. First, whether or not the justice's actions truly constituted impeachable offenses remains debatable today. Chief Justice Rehnquist interprets Chase's acquittal before the Senate as properly teaching that "removal of individual members of the Court because of their judicial philosophy is not permissible" and implies that the decision of the Senate was proper (quoted in Rehnquist 1992, 134). Raoul Berger's (1974) study of Chase's trial led him to the opposite conclusion: Chase's behavior did constitute impeachable offenses. That disagreement underscores the difficulties involved in imputing motives and analyzing the validity of prosecutorial or congressional assessments: were the judges targeted because of their venality or other ethical failings or because of their judicial philosophies?

Simple mathematical calculations clarify the rationale for the rash of House investigations and impeachments in the early twentieth century. Impeachment votes on four judges in the House of Representatives followed party lines; Senate decisions on removal, however, did not. The tactic of merely beginning an investigation in the House as a spur to the judge's resignation was far more effective, and seven Republican judges left the bench in advance of formal impeachment.

How the executive branch has wielded its prosecutorial power to rid the bench of undesirable judges also requires a complicated calculus. If all of the judges who were subjected to criminal investigations were indeed guilty of corrupt practices, then the executive branch was not attempting to influence the ideological composition of the bench. Four judges who were prosecuted and convicted during the Reagan and Bush administrations could each point to at least one specific anti-government decision he had rendered that blocked an administration policy. The validity of either view remains, however, in the eye of the beholder.

SEPARATION OF POWERS PERSPECTIVE

Analysis of judicial impeachment historically is riddled with holes if one attempts to impute specific motives and discern actual culpability in each case.

The lessons drawn are contradictory and inevitably rely on incomplete informa-tion. Each individual case can be judged only in its limited historical epoch. For that reason, viewing the impeachment process as part of a larger game of separa-tion of powers allows for more dispassionate consideration, not only of what has occurred but also of motives that transcend those of simple partisanship.

What Congress wants from judges is that legislative bargains be faithfully applied, and the executive wants to faithfully execute the law or to attain that branch's policy goals through the courts. These goals are only assured on if judges are reliable. Put differently, the executive and legislative branches want the freedom to assume that the legal model, whereby judges seek only legal clarity and legal accuracy in their opinions, prevails. A side note to that assertion is that legislators and presidents really want judges to reach legally clear and accurate conclusions that are consistent with those of a majority of senators and representatives or with the president. All three branches also share the goal of maintaining regime legiti-macy, which is compromised when judges forfeit impartiality or behave corruptly.

Judicial reliability wanes, in other words, when judges exercise their own dis-cretion in pursuit of their own policy preferences or make decisions colored by money, self-interest, or other suspect motives. Therefore, whether judges are investigated or impeached for ethical lapses or for furthering their own policy goals becomes irrelevant. Either incentive renders the judges unreliable from the perspective of the other powers of government. The reason for the judge's inter-fering with executive or legislative goals becomes inconsequential when the incentive for altering the judge's behavior or removing the unreliable jurist is viewed as a strategy in pursuit of policy goals. Executive or legislative actions aimed at a single judge are also presumed to have a ripple effect on other judges, as the message flows outward in concentric circles. Maintaining regime legiti-macy from taint by unreliable judicial pronouncements merely reinforces the original political goal for instituting a judicial branch: judges enforce the bar-gains struck by other parts of government.

Seen in this light, all of the judges who were investigated, prosecuted, or impeached had exhibited a form of unreliability. They acted in some fashion that failed to conform to pacts negotiated or threatened regime stability through improprieties. Pickering's and Chase's ideological persuasion made them unde-sirable; the same was true for six others who were subjected to congressional investigations by Jeffersonian Democrats. Similarly, the seven judges investigated and four impeached in the first three decades of the twentieth century were, save one, of the opposite political affiliation of that dominant in the House of Representatives. In the last decades, Republican executives prosecuted five judges, all but one of whom were Democrats.

The proposition that partisan ideology was the determining factor in all attempts to curb judicial unreliability breaks down, though, when impeachments reached the Senate. Chase (1805), Swayne (1904), and Louderback (1933) were all acquitted, despite the partisan make-up of the Senate. Perhaps the legal trappings that surround the Senate, sitting as judge and jury, imbued that chamber with a less partisan atmosphere. Or, maybe, nothing more solemn than the requirement of a super-majority of two-thirds to convict saved four unreliable judges from removal.

Viewing legislative and executive attempts to unseat judges as prompted by a judge's behaving unreliably also enables one to move beyond the narrow confines of the United States and to look more broadly at how and why judges may be sanctioned. Judicial power around the world is expanding (Tate and Vallinder 1995). In a rationally organized world, there is a proportional relationship between power and responsibility, and, thus, as the power of judges increases, so too is the expectation of enlarged responsibility (Cappelletti 1983). The American scheme places monitoring judicial responsibility in the hands of the executive and Congress, but other nations have sought other locations for that function. There is, all too often, minimal accountability for judges (Volcansek, de Franciscis, and Lafon 1996). Cross-nationally the force of history, culture, and tradition also mold different expectations for judicial comportment. In one study of Western democracies, three broad categories of inappropriate behavior were isolated: political corruption, personal corruption, and bringing disrepute upon the judiciary (Volcansek, de Franciscis, and Lafon 1996). On closer inspection, each of these forms of judicial misconduct that could bring official sanctions on judges could easily be subsumed under the rubric of judicial unreliability.

Judicial unreliability is the price of judicial independence. An independent judiciary is touted by some democratization theorists as an essential characteristic of a democratic regime, but the nature of that independence is often ill defined. "In practice," according to Mény and Knapp (1998, 318), "there never was a truly independent judiciary." The confusion usually resides in separating clearly institutional independence from personal independence; the former typically connotes an absence of direct influence on judicial decisions by other branches of government or other sources of power. Complete personal autonomy for any judge is not a requirement for an independent judiciary, but a number of the judges who were investigated, prosecuted, or impeached in American history did not seemingly recognize limits to their own actions, on and off the bench. Indeed, judges are generally subjected to higher standards of personal conduct than are other political officeholders, and a single ethical lapse by a judge prompts a totally disproportionate response (Volcansek, de Franciscis, and Lafon 1996).

In separation of powers games, however, judicial independence is what stymies the goals of legislatures and executives and is also the source of much judicial prerogative. Lip service is paid to the value of an independent judicial branch that "preserve[s] property rights and contract," (quoted Hix 1999, 103) but that independence does not exist in isolation from politics (Mény and Knapp 1998). Judges' reputation for strict neutrality is central to the social legitimacy of the system (Stone Sweet 2000), but in the world of practical politics, the lawmakers and presidents expect judges to ratify and enforce their political agendas.

A modified version of Weingast's separation of powers model, in which the whole federal judiciary is represented and in which judges, as well as legislators and presidents, anticipate the reactions of the other players, enables us to capture the tensions inherent in a scheme of divided institutional government. It can illustrate the paradox of judicial politics between enforcing collective decisions or legislative–executive bargains and judicial independence (Hix 1999). The game is dynamic and never fixed; the judges speak, but their pronouncements can be overridden or the judges are individually brought to account. More important, it underscores that in a separation of powers game, judges are players, but in some sense "elected politicians always have the 'last word' "(Mény and Knapp 1998, 321). Unreliable judges can be brought to heel or removed.

CHAPTER FOUR

Congress and the Court: The Strange Case of Census 2000

THOMAS L. BRUNELL

Article I, section 2 of the U.S. Constitution reads in part, "The actual Enumeration shall be made within three Years after the first Meeting of Congress of the United States, and within every subsequent Term of ten Years, in such Manner as they shall be Law direct." While originally the decennial census was used for both reapportionment and for levying taxes on the basis of the states' population share, the modern census has been incorporated into the redistricting process (for both congressional and state legislative districts) as well as the distribution of federal funds. The modern usage of the census necessitates highly accurate data at very low levels of geography—down to even the household level. Census 2000 has been extremely visible in part because the two political parties have been waging a fierce war over exactly how to conduct the census itself. The battle has been over whether or not to incorporate statistical sampling in the calculation of the population of the country.[1] While the battle over Census 2000 has probably been the most visible yet, a number of scuffles over the 1990 census occurred as well (Anderson 1988; Hogan 1993; Breiman 1994; Anderson and Fienberg 1999; Stark 1999; Brown, et al. 1999; Brunell forthcoming 2000).

In *Department of Commerce v. U.S. House of Representatives* (1999) the Supreme Court by a five-to-four decision prohibited the use of statistical sampling in calculating the population for purposes of apportionment. The Court's decision, as explained in detail below, was based on statutory interpretation of congressional legislation. This decision is significant because it overruled the use of sampling techniques designed to the undercounting of children, minorities, and the poor.

While much of this battle has occurred inside the Capitol, the courts have already played, and will continue to play, an important role in determining how the census ought to be done. The relationship between Congress and the Court on this particular issue is fascinating, in part, because the Supreme Court was put in a position of stepping in the middle of an intractable political dispute between the executive and legislative branches. Further, the "typical" view of the role that the court plays in the American political process does not apply. The courts were not relegated to merely interpreting the laws that Congress had written. In this case, some members of Congress, in particular the Republican leadership, saw the judicial branch as an outlet for one prong of their overall strategy to affect the disposition of the census.

WHAT'S WRONG WITH THE CENSUS?

Simply put, the decennial census does not accurately count all inhabitants of the country. Of late, the net undercount has been somewhere in the neighborhood of 2 percent of the population. This fact, in and of itself, would not pose a problem if those missed were distributed randomly across states, ethnicities, genders, etc. Unfortunately, this is not the case. Minorities, residents of the inner city, and people who rent their homes are missed more often than others (Anderson and Feinberg 1999). This is clearly unfair and ought to be resolved. The Census Bureau devised a plan to rectify this situation. It sought use of statistical sampling in two new and controversial ways to adjust the census.

The Census Bureau proposed to alter the method of census taking in two important ways. First, it wanted to take a sample of households that failed to respond to the census via mail. Second, it wanted to incorporate a follow-up survey to adjust census population figures for people who were missed (and double counted) in the census itself. I outline in detail both of these proposals later in the chapter.

While the redistricting process always promises to be a hard-fought partisan battle, with much of the fighting done in the courtroom, the upcoming round may turn out to be the fiercest battle yet. In addition to the vague guidelines set by *Shaw v. Reno* (1993), all parties involved will also have to contend with two different sets of data from the Census Bureau. Census data are the standard by which the House of Representatives is apportioned as well as the basis for redistricting federal and state legislative districts.

Indeed, the battle lines for the 2000 redistricting round were taking shape by the mid-1990s. It is then that the Democrats and Republicans began to square off over the method to be used in the upcoming census. Both parties see the census as directly affecting the number of seats they may win in the House of Representatives. Democrats and Republicans alike are assuming that an adjusted census will count more minorities and this, in turn, will help the Democrats win more seats. In this chapter I describe the debate over statistical adjustment and explain how we have arrived at the point where the Bureau will release two sets of population data and then assess the likely impact this will have on the redrawing of district lines.

TO ADJUST OR NOT?

The decennial census has been the subject of intense scrutiny and debate mainly because the modern census is not a whole lot different from the method used in the nineteenth century. Today we hear the cry for a census that uses "modern scientific methods," and while the statistical methods are really not all that modern, they may solve some of the ills suffered by the census.

What's the problem with the census? Well, the census misses millions of people in an effort to count each person in America.[2] But the simple fact that the census misses millions of people is not the problem. If the people missed were undercounted randomly across states, ethnicities, and age groups, the undercount would not be problematic. Unfortunately, they are not. There is a systematic bias or a differential undercount in the census. Blacks, Hispanics, American Indians, poor people, and urban residents are all missed at higher rates than other residents are. Table 4.1 reports the final estimates[3] for the undercount by ethnicity. The total estimates' net undercount for the nation was 1.58 percent.

The Initial Plan

The original plan had two controversial aspects that involved statistical sampling. The first aspect involved the use of sampling for nonresponse follow-up (SNRFU). In an effort to save both time and money the Census Bureau wanted to implement a plan whereby only a sample of those households that do not

TABLE 4.1 ESTIMATED UNDERCOUNT BY ETHNICITY IN 1990 CENSUS

Group	Estimated Undercount (%)
U.S. Total	1.58
Black	4.43
Asian/Pacific Islander	2.33
American Indian/Eskimo	4.52
Hispanic	4.96

Source: Report of the Committee on Adjustment of Postcensal Estimates (August 1992), 3.

respond via sending their census form by mail will be visited by an actual enumerator. Traditionally, any household that does not respond by mail is slated for a visit by a census enumerator. With declining participation in the census, nonresponse follow-up becomes more expensive and time consuming. The second aspect of the plan involved a coverage evaluation survey that is designed to adjust population tallies at all levels of geography. Originally called the Integrated Coverage Measurement (ICM) the survey was re-designed and renamed after the Supreme Court ruling. The survey is now called the Accuracy and Coverage Evaluation (ACE).

Sampling for Nonresponse Follow-up (SNRFU)

In conducting the enumeration process, the Census Bureau first sends out census forms to each and every household in the United States for which it has an address.[4] The majority of households across the country mail back their completed forms (recently around two out of three people nationally).[5] For those households that do not respond via the mail, the Bureau hires hundreds of thousands of temporary employees to visit each of the nonresponding households in order to collect the appropriate data. Even after this monumental task, in no census has every person actually been counted; erroneous enumerations always exist, people are missed altogether, or people are counted twice. The key to understanding the "fix" that the Bureau has proposed is to first understand the problem. The problem *is not* that the census misses 2 percent of the population, indeed if we took a random sample of just 2 percent of the population we would know a great deal about it. If that 2 percent were randomly distributed across states, ethnicities, ages, sexes, etc. it would not matter. The errors made by the census are systematic. They tend to miss people who are poor, minorities, and people who rent rather than own their house.

For the 2000 census the Bureau proposes bypassing a portion of those households that do not respond to the census by mail (about 11 million), thereby reducing its workload and expense. The plan (see Table 4.2) works as follows: take a sample for each census tract (about 1,700 households) so that the total number of households for which data will be collected will equal 90 percent. Thus, if 50 percent of the households in a census tract respond by mail, the Bureau will visit just four out of the five households that did not respond. If the mail-back response rate is 80 percent the Bureau will visit one out of every two households that did not respond. The 10 percent of the households that both did not respond by mail and were not visited by an enumerator will be imputed based on the sample of households that did not respond but were visited by an enumerator. Thus, if the Smiths did not mail back their form and were not part of the sample for nonresponse follow-up they are part of the "10 percent setaside." Data on demographics and number of members of the Smith household,

TABLE 4.2 NONRESPONSE FOLLOW-UP SAMPLING PLAN

Initial Mail-back Response Rate (%)	Sampling Rate
50	4 in 5
60	3 in 4
70	2 in 3
80	1 in 2
85 or higher	1 in 3

as shown in the sampling plan, will be imputed from the nearest household that did not mail back its form, but was visited by a census enumerator.[6]

The Coverage Evaluation Survey

Originally called the Integrated Coverage Measurement (ICM), the coverage evaluation survey is designed to measure as a characteristic how well the census counted portions of the population. While the Census Bureau has conducted these surveys to evaluate how well the census has done in prior years, it has never used the data to then adjust population totals. This adjustment is the centerpiece of the fight between the political parties. Simply put, the Census Bureau's original plans included conducting a follow-up survey of 750,000 households in order to check how well the census itself measured the population. The generic name for this method is the "capture-recapture model." The specific details of the plan will be covered in depth later in the chapter. First, we need to turn to the Supreme Court ruling of January 1999.

THE COURT CASES

In late 1997 the U.S. House of Representatives addressed the census issue when it took up the annual appropriations bill for the Departments of Commerce, Justice, and State. The Republican-led House wanted to make it difficult or impossible for the Census Bureau to use statistical sampling. The Democrats resisted these efforts. Eventually a compromise was reached that allowed for the Census Bureau to prepare for a census that included statistical sampling, but the agreement also let the Republicans challenge this effort in court. The appropriations bill (which became Public Law 105-119) declared "that it shall be the duty of a district court hearing an action under this section and the Supreme Court to advance on the docket and expedite the disposition of any such matter" (Sec. 209). It also explicitly allowed the Speaker of the House to "commence or join in a civil action to prevent the use of any statistical method in connection with the decennial census" (Sec. 209).

Two cases were filed—one by Newt Gingrich, who was Speaker of the House at that time, and the other by a group of sixteen individuals that were organized by a conservative interest group based in Atlanta, Georgia—the Southeastern Legal Foundation. A special three-judge panel heard each case. Both cases were decided unanimously on summary judgment in favor of the Republicans (i.e., the cases ruled that statistical sampling was illegal for use in the decennial census). The Supreme Court agreed to review the decisions.

The Supreme Court

On November 30, 1998, the Supreme Court heard oral arguments on *Department of Commerce v. U.S. House of Representatives* (1999). The two lower court cases were enjoined by the Supreme Court and heard as a single case.[7] Maureen Mahoney argued the bulk of the case for the House of Representatives. Justice Scalia in particular questioned her at length as to whether there existed a precedent for the Court to intervene between the executive and legislative branches to resolve what is essentially a political dispute. Scalia suggested that Ms. Mahoney cite a case that the Court decided involving the president and Congress. She tried, among others, *United States v. Nixon* (1974) and *Immigration and Naturalization Service v. Chadha* (1983). Justice Scalia felt that none of these cases was sufficiently similar to what the Court was being asked to address in the case before it. Scalia remarked: "I don't like injecting us [the Supreme Court] into a battle between the two political branches. I think they will survive. I am not sure we will."

Solicitor General Seth Waxman argued the case for the administration. He said that the House should not be permitted to accomplish through litigation what it could not achieve by legislation, a point with which justices sympathetic to both sides appeared inclined to agree. Justice Ruth Bader Ginsberg agreed with Scalia's position when she characterized Congress's position as: "Gee, this is really important, and we want you to resolve this."

Later, Scalia suggested that if Congress does not agree with the president on this issue it should just not appropriate money to staff the White House, which would result in a governmental shutdown restricted to 1600 Pennsylvania Avenue. While this sounds like a novel approach to resolve executive–legislative relations, it must strike most political observers as an impractical solution. Nonetheless, the justice's comments are indicative of the fact that some on the Court felt that this was a political issue and should be solved by the executive and legislative branches.

Later the questions turned to reasonable methods of census taking. In response to a question that asked what a census taker should do if he is certain someone lives in a house but is unwilling to answer the door, Mahoney felt the appropriate action was to record zero people living at that address. "Your Honor, they [the census enumerators] can't guess," Ms. Mahoney responded to a question as to the appropriate way to enumerate a house that appeared to be occupied. She went on to indicate that a non-responding household should be counted as having zero people living there. A good deal of the line of questioning also addressed the constitutional and statutory language applicable to the census.

The Supreme Court Decision

On January 25, 1999, the Supreme Court released its decision on the two cases brought before it regarding the use of statistical sampling in the decennial census. Simply put, the Court ruled that, at least for the purposes of apportionment, the Census Bureau might not use statistical sampling in calculating the population of each of the states. Justice O'Connor in her majority opinion wrote that section 195 of the Census Act (Title 13, United States Code) "prohibits the proposed uses of statistical sampling in calculating the population for purposes of apportionment." The decision was based on the Census Act in which Congress granted authority to the Secretary of Commerce to conduct the decennial census.[8] The case was in response to two cases filed in early 1998 challenging the legality of using sampling in the census. Both cases were heard by federal three-judge panels; both panels voted unanimously that the Census Bureau's sampling plan violated the Census Act and permanently enjoined the planned use of sampling in the decennial reapportionment process.

While much of the coverage and discussion as to the constitutionality of the use of sampling given the phrase "actual enumeration" in the U.S. Constitution (Article I, section 2), all of the court cases were decided on statutory grounds rather than constitutional grounds. There are two relevant sections of Title 13 that apply. First, §141(a):

> (a) The Secretary [of Commerce] shall, in the year 1980 and every 10 years thereafter, take a decennial census of population as of the first day of April of such year, which date shall be known the "decennial census date," in such form and content as he may determine, including the use of sampling procedures and special surveys. (13 U.S.C. §141[a])

and §195:

> Except for the determination of population for purposes of apportionment of Representatives in Congress among the several States, the Secretary shall, if he considers it feasible, authorize the use of the statistical method know as "sampling" in carrying out the provisions of this title. (13 U.S.C. §195)

The dissenting justices' interpretation: "They authorize sampling in both the decennial and the mid-decade census, but they only command its use when the determination is not for apportionment purposes" (*Department of Commerce v. U.S. House of Representatives* 1999, 3). The majority opinion interprets the second section as expressly prohibiting the Secretary of Commerce from using sampling when determining population for the purposes of apportionment. Nonetheless, the Court spoke and the decision forced the Census Bureau to reevaluate its plans for the 2000 census. However, the decision was not a clear-cut victory for Republicans or Democrats.

Both political parties had something to smile about. The Democrats were relieved because the Court did not rule that statistical sampling could not be used for redistricting or the distribution of federal funds. The Republicans had something to be happy about as well—the Court agreed that, in part, sampling was not allowed under the current law. Further, the ruling made it necessary that the Census Bureau calculate the population without a statistical adjustment. Therefore, the country will be left with two sets of census data—the unadjusted enumeration data and the data that will be adjusted using the follow-up survey.

The Revised Plan

The decision by the Supreme Court that outlaws use of statistical sampling for purposes of apportionment allowed some revisions in the plan. First, SNRFU had to be scrapped. Clearly, the Bureau could not follow up on only a portion of the households that failed to respond by mail. It would have to conduct 100 percent follow-up. This however was only part of the picture. SNRFU was simply a way to save time and money, but it is through the coverage evaluation survey that the Democrats and all those who supported a census correction could adjust population figures. The Court's ruling said nothing about the plan to conduct the survey or adjust the official census data for purposes of federal funding and redistricting. The ruling did affect the follow-up survey somewhat in that the Census Bureau changed the sample size from 750,000 households to 300,000 households.[9] It also renamed this portion of the plan from the ICM to the ACE.

The ACE measures the coverage of the census itself. It gives us an idea about how well different groups of people were counted in the first place. That is, the Census Bureau will derive estimates of the undercount (overcount) for discrete groups of people. For instance, it is designed to discern how well people are counted in terms of their age, gender, area of the country, and ethnicity.

While the Republicans were hoping for a grand slam with the court ruling, they had to settle for a bloop single.[10] The three major programs that are affected by the census data are: reapportionment, redistricting, and the distribution of some federal funding. While the national parties may care at some level about the distribution of seats among the states, clearly the issue both parties are genuinely concerned about is the redistricting process. The door was left open to use the survey portion of the plan in order to adjust the population tallies at all levels of geography.

THE "NEW" CENSUS

The best way to understand the new plan is to think of the census in two phases: the enumeration phase where the Bureau attempts to count 100 percent of population; and the ACE in which a follow-up survey of 300,000 households will be conducted. Briefly, the ACE will be used to adjust the population totals by specific post-strata or groups (i.e., renters/owners, race and ethnicity, age, and sex). Before explaining the details of how this adjustment will take place, let's outline how this capture-recapture method works.

Say, for example, one wants to estimate the number of fish in a lake—using the capture-recapture method you would: catch some fish, tag them, and put them back in the lake (say one thousand fish); wait a day in order to let the tagged and untagged fish mix; or catch another set of fish and count the number with tags (say eighty tagged, twenty untagged). The number of untagged fish in the second catch is an estimate of the proportion of fish missed. In other words, the estimate of the total population is the number of fish in the first catch/fraction of tagged fish in the second catch. So in our example: 1,000/.80 = 1,250 fish in the lake.

This plan rests on a number of important assumptions. First, each fish must have the same probability of being caught. Second, the fish should mix randomly between catches. Third, the number of fish in the lake should be constant between catches. And four, the tagged fish need to remain tagged. Unfortunately, this simple approach does not work in the census. Rather than tagging individuals, the Bureau relies on matching names and addresses. Roughly, the approach for the census would be: to take the census; to take a stratified random sample of 300,000 households and recount them; to figure out how many people were missed and how many were counted erroneously; or to adjust the population figures stratum by stratum based on this information.

At some point before census day, the Census Bureau will choose a stratified random sample of 300,000 households. The Bureau will then revisit each of these households (after the initial headcount portion of the census is over) in an attempt to recollect information from each of them. After this is done there are two sets of data for these 300,000 households: the initial headcount, and the ACE survey. Now the Bureau can compare the 300,000 households from the ACE to the *same* set of households in the enumeration phase. This model is called the "capture-recapture" in the statistics literature[11] (see Model 4.1).

Theoretically, three of the four interior cells are observable. N_{22} (the "fourth cell") consists of those people not counted in either the census or the follow-up

Model 4.1

ACE	In	Out	Total
In	N_{11}	N_{12}	N_{1+}
Out	N_{21}	N_{22}	N_{2+}
Total	N_{+1}	N_{+2}	N_{++}

survey. However, we can still estimate the total population as: N_{++} = $(N_{+1})(N_{+1})/N_{11}$.[12] This is called a dual system estimator (Hogan 1993; Waite and Hogan 1998). For each individual post-stratum, a separated dual system estimator will be calculated. Then the estimated population can be compared to the population counts from the census. The ratio of the dual system estimator to the true population is the adjustment factor for that post-stratum.[13]

This sampling model, like all statistical models, makes some assumptions. The assumption of constant undercount rates within a population is called the homogeneity assumption and violations of this assumption are called heterogeneity. In order to reduce the effects of heterogeneity bias, the Bureau puts each person into a unique post-stratum. Clearly, we know that the probability of being enumerated is correlated with demographic data like ethnicity, income, and whether one rents or owns his place of residence (Hogan 1993; Waite and Hogan 1998). In order to reduce the variability in capture probability (the likelihood of being enumerated) each person is classified into one of the unique post-strata defined by the following variables:[14]

Age/Sex—Seven post-strata
0–17 Male and Female; 18–29 Male; 18–29 Female; 30–49 Male; 30–49 Female; 50+ Male; 50+ Female

Race/Ethnicity—Five post-strata
Hispanic; Non-Hispanic White & other; Non-Hispanic Black; Non-Hispanic Asian & Pacific Islander; Non-Hispanic American Indian/Alaskan Native

Tenure—Two post-strata
Own or Rent

Region—Four post-strata
West: Alaska, Arizona, California, Colorado, Hawaii, Idaho, Montana, Nevada, New Mexico, Oregon, Utah, Washington, and Wyoming
Midwest: Illinois, Indiana, Iowa, Kansas, Michigan, Minnesota, Missouri, Nebraska, North Dakota, Ohio, South Dakota, and Wisconsin

South: Alabama, Arkansas, Delaware, District of Colombia, Florida, Georgia, Kentucky, Louisiana, Maryland, Mississippi, North Carolina, Oklahoma, South Carolina, Tennessee, Texas, Virginia, and West Virginia

Northeast: Connecticut, Maine, Massachusetts, New Hampshire, New Jersey, New York, Pennsylvania, Rhode Island, and Vermont

Urban/Rural—Three post-strata

Urban areas greater than 250,000; Other urban; Rural

Say that Charlie was out of town on vacation on April 1, 2000, and is not included in the initial headcount. However, on the follow-up ACE portion of the census he is counted. The Census Bureau knows that Charlie was part of the undercount because he should have been counted and was not. Based upon this information, the Bureau infers, in a statistical sense, that other people (hundreds of other people) just like Charlie must also have been missed. Based on the number of people (and their demographic characteristics) missed the Bureau will adjust the number of people in each census block.[15] Thus the country will be left with two separate and different numbers: one unadjusted set to be used for reapportionment and one adjusted set that the Bureau will argue is much more accurate to be used for federal funding and redistricting.

IMPLICATIONS FOR REDISTRICTING

The question for the upcoming round of redistricting will be: should a state use the adjusted figures or unadjusted (enumeration) data? The Census Bureau will be releasing both sets of numbers, although there may be a chance that one set will be "official" and the other will just be released. Uncertainty remains high over the outcome of the 2000 census and how the data will look. Further, the elections in November 2000, especially the presidential race, also play an important role in what comes to pass.

Two Numbers

In *Karcher v. Daggett* (1983) the Supreme Court ruled that "the census count provides the only reliable—albeit less than perfect—indication of the districts' 'real' relative population levels, and furnishes the only basis for good-faith attempts to achieve population equality." The problem then becomes which set of census data is more accurate? Both sides will be lining up expert witnesses to testify on this very issue. The Republicans will likely mount a two-pronged attack: first, disputing the constitutionality and legality of the adjusted data; second, arguing that the adjusted data can be less accurate, especially at smaller levels of geography.

Does the phrase "actual enumeration" require a headcount? Although Justice Scalia's concurring opinion clearly indicates that at least he would rule that an "actual enumeration" meant a census without sampling, "[t]he notion of counting 'singly,' 'separately,' 'number by number,' 'distinctly,' which runs through these definitions is incompatible (or at least arguably incompatible, which is all that needs to be established) with gross statistical estimates" (*Department of Commerce v. U.S. House of Representatives* 1999, 15). But one justice does not a majority make.

The second argument from the anti-adjustment side is that the lowest levels of geography (i.e., city, county, and block levels), when adjusted through statistics, makes population totals less accurate than the unadjusted totals. The argument is straightforward in terms of any technique that uses statistical inference. The adjustment will make corrections on average, however; if one looks at a specific tract or block of homes the correction will not always improve accuracy and sometimes it will lessen the accuracy of the census itself.

Lawsuits and Section 5 of the Voting Rights Act

The redistricting lawsuits surrounding the use of data from the 2000 census have already begun. Under section 5 of the Voting Rights Act there are nine whole states and parts of seven others that must get administrative pre-clearance for state laws that change "standard, practice, or procedure with respect to voting" (42 U.S.C. §1973c.). Arizona recently enacted a state law that prohibits the state from using the adjusted census data in determining state and congressional districts. However, Arizona is one of the seven states that must get Department of Justice pre-clearance for any law affecting redistricting in the state and it has submitted its state law for such approval. In July 1999 the Department of Justice notified Arizona that it must provide support for its contention that prohibiting the use of adjusted census data will not hurt minorities in the state.

Alaska, like Arizona, passed a state law in May 1999 that prohibits the use of adjusted census data for the purposes of redistricting. Alaska is also covered under section 5 and the May 1999 state law must be pre-cleared by the Department of Justice or a special three-judge count in Washington, D.C.

Two other states have also passed into law provisions that require the state to use the enumeration data rather than the adjusted numbers. Colorado passed Senate bill 206 and it was signed into law on May 5, 1999. In that bill one of the justifications for using the enumeration data is that it "would subject the state of Colorado to the risk of litigation over the appropriate population figures, which form the very foundation of any congressional or state legislative redistricting plan" (section 1, paragraph h). Colorado will undoubtedly be sued over the use of unadjusted data as well.

Kansas has also passed a state law requiring the use of unadjusted data in the next round of redistricting. Kansas is the only state to adjust the federal census figures used for redistricting. The state adjustment counts military personnel and college students in their hometowns rather than where they were when the census was taken.[16] In 1988, Kansas's voters approved a constitutional amendment requiring the adjustment of federal census figures for reapportionment. One commonality shared by these four states is that the Republicans control the executive and both chambers of the state legislatures in each state. What is as of yet unclear is whether or not these laws will be upheld in court.

REDISTRICTING IN THE "AUGHTS"

In terms of the partisan majority status in the House of Representatives, state legislative and gubernatorial races are even more important in the year 2000 than any House race in the country. The head of the Republican redistricting office, Tom Hofeller, certainly feels that way. "The gerrymander trumps all else. The parties have to be looking closely at state level elections for November 2000" (author's interview, September 17, 1999). It is in these races that the parties may best situate themselves for the next round of redistricting. The battle for control of House of Representatives over the next decade is going to be decided in state legislative and gubernatorial elections in the year 2000.

While it is difficult to predict which party will have the upper hand in terms of the number of states for which it controls the redistricting process, we can get some idea from the current balance of power. Table 4.3 lists the number of House seats in each state, which party controlled redistricting in the 1990s, and which party would control in 2000 if the composition of the state government remains unchanged after the 2000 election.

The news for each party is mixed. For the GOP, the up-side is that fact that it has increased its control over state governments significantly: it would control the line drawing for ten states with 113 seats compared to only two states with five seats in the 1990 round. Positive for the Democrats is that they still control the map-making process for more seats (thirteen states with 144 seats) than the Republicans do in the upcoming round. Clearly the momentum is with the GOP—there are significantly fewer states that have divided control now relative to 1990, and nearly all of those changes have been in favor of the Republicans. Again, the table is predicated on the current balance of power, and things can and perhaps will change after the upcoming election.

If the adjusted data are used, as it will be in some states, what kind of effect can we expect? It is likely to deliver a few more seats to the Democrats, something on the order of five seats, but certainly not a watershed of twenty to thirty seats. The adjusted census will pick up more minorities than an unadjusted

TABLE 4.3 PARTY CONTROL OF REDISTRICTING IN 1991 AND 2001

State	Seats	Position in 1991					Status Quo for 2001				
		At-L	Rep	Dem	Split	Com	At-L	Rep	Dem	Split	Com
Alabama	7			7					7		
Alaska	1	1					1				
Arizona	8				6			8			
Arkansas	4			4					4		
California	53				52				53		
Colorado	7				6			7			
Connecticut	5				6					5	
Delaware	1	1					1				
Florida	24			23				24			
Georgia	13			11					13		
Hawaii	2					2					2
Idaho	2				2						2
Illinois	19				20					19	
Indiana	10			10					10		
Iowa	5				5					5	
Kansas	4				4			4			
Kentucky	6			6						6	
Louisiana	7			7						7	
Maine	2				2					2	
Maryland	8			8					8		
Massachusetts	10				10				10		
Michigan	16				16			16			
Minnesota	8				8					8	
Mississippi	4			5					4		
Missouri	9				9				9		
Montana	1	1					1				
Nebraska	3				3			3			
Nevada	3			2						3	
New Hampshire	2		2							2	
New Jersey	13			13							13
New Mexico	3			3						3	
New York	29				31					29	
North Carolina	12			12					12		
North Dakota	1	1					1				
Ohio	18				19			18			
Oklahoma	5			6						5	
Oregon	5				5					5	

continued

TABLE 4.3 *CONTINUED*

State	Seats	Position in 1991					Status Quo for 2001				
		At-L	Rep	Dem	Split	Com	At-L	Rep	Dem	Split	Com
Pennsylvania	19			21				19			
Rhode Island	2			2					2		
South Carolina	6			6						6	
South Dakota	1	1					1				
Tennessee	9			9					9		
Texas	32			30						32	
Utah	3		3					3			
Vermont	1	1					1				
Virginia	11			11				11			
Washington	9					9					9
West Virginia	3			3					3		
Wisconsin	8			9						8	
Wyoming	1	1					1				
Totals	435	7	5	172	240	11	7	113	144	145	26

Note: The table lists how many House seats are controlled by each party in terms of the upcoming round of redistricting compared to the 1990 round. Those states with entries under *Rep* or *Dem* indicate that a single party controls the state government. *At-L* are at-large states (1 seat) and *Com* indicates redistricting is done by a commission.

census. But the addition of a few hundred or even a few thousand people in a city will be negligible. In order for the Democrats to gain seats with great certainty the additional people need to be greatly concentrated. Thus, the areas in which we should see the most significant changes will be in urban districts. In those districts the physical size will shrink, because more people will be found in the inner city, and this will have a spill-over effect outward. The size of the spillover will determine whether or not the Democrats can draw additional districts or redraw an existing district more favorably.

CONCLUSION

For a state to completely avoid redistricting lawsuits, at this point, is nearly unimaginable. Since there will be two sets of data, this gives every party who might already be planning to sue, another justifiable reason to file a lawsuit. In the game of redistricting the goal from the outset is not to avoid litigation, rather it is to set oneself up to win the inevitable lawsuits. The upcoming round of redistricting should be, by all measures, the fiercest, most partisan battle yet.

There are at least three factors contributing to this: the data issue, the blurry racial guidelines from *Shaw v. Reno* (1993), and the bare majority in the U.S. House of Representatives.

While the outcome of this particular census is still uncertain in terms of the statistical adjustment issue, we can be certain that the battle will not end with this census either. However, one thing is for certain, this issue will be brought up again (and again) in dozens of lawsuits during the upcoming round of redistricting. The decisions that are made over the next few years will not only directly affect the make-up of the House of Representatives and state legislatures across the country, but they may help define the appropriate methodology for fixing the decennial census in the year 2010.

NOTES

1. I will not address an equally important and contentious census issue—multiracial categories. Census 2000 is also the first time that a person may mark more than one racial category. This has important implications for how to count racial minorities, which directly affects redistricting.

2. Actually, the census does not simply tally the number of people in the country; it must also record exactly where each individual lives in the country as well.

3. I say "final estimates" because they did change considerably. The original estimate was a 2.08 percent undercount for the nation and was later revised as the statistical model used to create these estimates was changed.

4. The Bureau has updated and continually updates the Master Address File (MAF).

5. The Census Bureau is forecasting a 61 percent mail-back return rate for 2000.

6. This process is called systematic hot deck imputation. Again the process is to just assign the characteristics of a known household to the household where we have no actual data.

7. *Department of Commerce v. House of Representatives*, 525 US 316 (1999), and *Clinton v. Glavin*, 525 US 959 (1998).

8. Another important argument in both cases had to do with whether or not the parties suing had standing. The Supreme Court felt that on the basis of possible vote dilution due to the loss of a seat in the House of Representatives, a resident of the state of Indiana had standing to sue since this loss would be directly related to whether or not sampling was used in the census.

9. The reason for this was that the ICM was to have separate post-strata for each individual state. That is, for the reapportionment of the House, the Bureau did not want to group data in the statistical adjustment process across state lines. Given that it now had to count (or try to count) all of the people, this type of grouping no longer made as much sense. Thus, the ACE will "borrow strength" across state boundaries—indeed the Bureau is considering eliminating the regional post-strata altogether.

10. In some sense it may have been a bigger victory than that since the Court's ruling does force the Census Bureau to attempt to count everyone, and this in turn made it possible for unadjusted data to be available for redistricting.

11. You capture part of a population once, then follow up with another capture. Now there are four types of individuals: 1) those who were in the first and the second sample (these people are "correctly enumerated"); 2) those who were in the first and not in the second (these people are called "unresolved"); 3) those not in the first but in the second (these people are the undercount); 4) those people missed in both the first and second phases.

12. This formula is the more standard notation of the example above. Both yield the same answer—in the example instead of 1,000/.80 = 1,250 we have (1,000*100)/80 = 1,250.

13. The actual formula for the dual system estimator for each post-stratum is as follows: (number of erroneous enumerations/census count)) * (survey count/number of matching records). Erroneous enumerations are those people miscounted (i.e., double counted, counted in a location where they should not have been, etc.). The census count is the raw number of people counted in the census phase of the enumeration process. The survey count is the number of people counted in the follow-up survey portion of the census. The number of matching records is the number of matches between the census and the survey—the number of people correctly counted.

14. These post-strata are subject to change. For instance, the Bureau is considering scrapping the regional post-strata in favor of a variable that takes into account the mail-back return rate. They state, "While the region is not entirely uncorrelated with undercount, we have become increasingly convinced that political geography, especially at such an aggregate level, is a poor predictor of either how census procedures are implemented or how people react to them. However our decision will be driven by the available data" (Hogan 2000 p. 21).

15. This process is actually done for each of the post-strata in the Census. Post-strata are simply groups of people lumped together because they share similar characteristics: Post-strata will be defined by age, sex, whether one rents or owns, race/ethnicity, and (perhaps) by the urbanization of the area you live in.

16. The Census Bureau counts people where they live for the majority of the year. So students are counted at their residence on campus rather than at home.

PART TWO

New Sources of Congressional–Judicial Confrontation

CHAPTER FIVE

How the Republican War over "Judicial Activism" Has Cost Congress

DAVID M. O'BRIEN

Congressional–judicial relations at the outset of the twenty-first century bear a resemblance to the antagonistic relationship between the federal judiciary and Congress at the end of the nineteenth century. Led by Chief Justice William H. Rehnquist, a bare majority of the Supreme Court and Republican appointees in the lower federal courts appears determined to limit Congress's lawmaking powers in defense of federalism and "states' sovereignty."

That Republican-appointed justices and judges are reclaiming federalism at the expense of Congress is clear not only from rulings in the 1990s, and the rhetoric in judicial opinions, striking down congressional statutes, but also in off-the-bench speeches and writings. For over a decade in his annual "Year-End Report of the Federal Judiciary," Chief Justice Rehnquist criticized Congress for expanding federal criminal law (Rehnquist 1999), implicitly inviting lower federal courts to invalidate congressional enactments, which they have done (*United States v. Morrison* 2000 and *Brzonkala v. Morrison* 1999, striking down the Violence Against Women Act of 1994). Nor is the chief justice alone in speaking out about federalism. Chief Judge J. Harvie Wilkinson III appointed to the U.S. Court of Appeals for the Fourth Circuit by Republican President Ronald Reagan, for one, applauds the Court's activism and concludes that, "The great contribution of the Rehnquist Court may be a 21st century change of national attitude toward the rightful roles of states" (Wilkinson 1999, A45; Greve 1999).

To put the realignment of institutional relations between Congress and the federal courts into historical perspective, recall that in the late nineteenth century and early twentieth century, the Court also sought to curb congressional power. The battle between the Court and Congress reached a head in the 1930s, when a bare majority of the Court struck down much of Democratic President Franklin D. Roosevelt's early New Deal legislation (*Schecter Poultry Corporation v. United States* 1935, invalidating the National Industrial Recovery Act of 1933). After winning a landslide reelection in 1936, FDR retaliated by proposing to increase the number of justices from nine to fifteen by appointing an additional justice for every one over age seventy, and thereby also securing a majority on the bench favorable to the New Deal. During the ensuing constitutional crisis in the spring of 1937 while the Senate debated FDR's plan, however, the Court handed down its famous "switch-in-time-that-saved-nine" decisions, abandoning its earlier doctrines limiting congressional power (*National Labor Relations Board v. Jones & Laughlin Steel Corporation* 1937; O'Brien 2000b). Subsequently, FDR's Court-packing plan was defeated and a much-chastened Court deferred to Congress on the scope of its lawmaking powers. Indeed, for almost fifty years the Court did not again curb Congress's power to regulate interstate commerce under Article I, or under its enforcement power of section 5 of the Fourteenth Amendment. As a result, a fairly stable body of constitutional doctrine and a pattern of judicial deference to Congress became established—established at least until the Rehnquist Court in the 1990s.

There is no little irony in the Rehnquist Court's curbing Congress in defense of the states, for after the 1994 midterm elections the Republican Party controlled both houses of Congress. Moreover, during the last thirty years Republican presidents—from Richard Nixon and Gerald Ford to Ronald Reagan and George Bush—appointed the overwhelming majority of the justices and lower court judges. Ironically, the realignment in congressional–judicial relations and the changing constitutional boundaries between congressional and state powers are rooted in how Republican presidents and members of Congress—especially senators—turned federal judgeships into symbols and instruments of their political power, imposing ever more ideological standards for judicial selection and polarizing the politics of Senate confirmation of judges.

The following section discusses how the politics of judicial appointments have been transformed due to Republican opposition to "judicial activism"—initially, opposition to the "liberal judicial activism" of the Warren Court (1953–1969) and to the Civil Rights Act of 1964 (enacted over "states' rights" objections under Congress's power to regulate interstate commerce and upheld in *Heart of Atlanta Motel v. United States* [1964]) and later, in the 1970s and 1980s, opposition to rulings on abortion (*Roe v. Wade* [1973]), affirmative action (*Regents of the University of California v. Bakke* [1978]; O'Brien 2000c), and busing (*Swann v. Charlotte-Mecklenberg Board of Education* [1971]). By the end of the 1980s, reversing those decisions and judicial appointments was a high (if not the highest) priority for social-conservative "movement" Republicans. The judicial appointments of Reagan and Bush went a long way toward transforming the judicial appointment process as well as the composition of the federal bench. Still, in the 1990s after losing access to presidential power and past influence on the selection of judicial nominees, movement conservatives stayed focused on federal judgeships and, indeed, increased pressure on moderate Republican senators in order to minimize the potential impact of judicial appointees of Democratic President Bill Clinton. As a result, Clinton was forced to abandon numerous judicial nominees and to trade judgeships with Republican senators in exchange for the Senate's confirmation of some judicial nominees (O'Brien 2000d; Alliance for Justice 1999). Together, these forces intensified an increasingly polarized judicial appointment process and contributed to the shifting direction of the judiciary.

After briefly discussing the transformation of the politics of judicial appointments, I turn to how the Rehnquist Court has been redefining the judiciary's relation to congressional power by redrawing the lines of power between Congress and the states.

TRANSFORMING THE POLITICS OF JUDICIAL APPOINTMENTS

The story of the transformation of the judicial appointment process might begin in the 1930s with FDR's appointees, followed by those of Democratic presidents Harry Truman, John F. Kennedy, and Lyndon B. Johnson. But those Democratic presidents neither gave judgeships a very high priority—instead, generally rewarding party faithful without scrutinizing their judicial philosophies—nor did they view judgeships as symbols and instruments of presidential power, as would later Republican presidents (O'Brien 2000e; O'Brien 1998; Goldman 1997). Furthermore, the transformation of the politics of judicial selection remains rooted in conservatives' opposition to the "liberal judicial activism" of the 1960s that contributed to Nixon's election and, subsequently, in the late 1970s and 1980s became identified with the New Right and Reagan Republicans.

Nixon won the 1968 presidential election with his famous "southern strategy" for winning over white Southern Democratic voters by denouncing "judicial activism," running a campaign based on restoring "law and order," and vowing to name only "strict constructionists" to the bench (Edsall and Edsall 1991; Rae 1989; Phillips 1970). Federal judgeships, thus, became political symbols in national electoral politics, and thereafter Republican presidential candidates have invariably made them an issue in their bids for the White House.

While Nixon made judgeships politically symbolic, however, he failed to impose the kind of rigorous judicial selection process that the Reagan administration would put into place in the 1980s. Furthermore, Nixon's four appointees to the Court (Chief Justice Warren E. Burger in 1969, Justice Harry A. Blackmun in 1970, and Justices Lewis F. Powell and Rehnquist in 1972), moved the Court in a more conservative direction on the rights of the accused, for example, but otherwise proved a disappointment for the emerging conservative Republican movement (O'Brien 2000e). The Burger Court (1969–1986) proclaimed a constitutional right for women to have abortions and upheld affirmative-action programs as well as busing to achieve integrated schools—precisely the issues that galvanized New Right conservatives in the 1980s and 1990s. In short, from the perspective of those later in the Reagan administration, Nixon's judges were largely lost opportunities and disappointments.

When Nixon was forced to resign in 1974, rather than face impeachment over his role in the Watergate cover-up, his successor, Gerald Ford, proved another disappointment for movement conservatives. Yet, as an unelected president, Ford was neither in a position to nominate controversial conservatives to the federal bench, nor was he disposed to do so. He delegated responsibility for judicial selection to his attorney general and generally named highly professional traditional Republicans. Ford's sole appointee to the Court—Justice John Paul Stevens in 1975—is illustrative: a moderate jurist inclined to self-restraint but without a clear agenda (O'Brien 1989a).

Republicans remained the minority party in Congress and, then, in the mid-1970s lost control of the White House for four years. Although Democratic President Jimmy Carter made no appointments to the Court, his administration further embittered conservative Republicans by reaching out to appoint non-traditional judges, such as women and African Americans (Goldman 1997).

Finally, with Reagan's election in 1980, movement conservatives had a White House committed to turning judgeships into not merely political symbols, but instruments of political power. Through the appointment of judges, as Attorney General Edwin Meese III declared, the administration aimed "to institutionalize the Reagan revolution so it can't be set aside no matter what happens in future presidential elections" (O'Brien 1988, 60, 63). It did so by putting into place the most rigorous and decidedly ideological judicial screening process ever. Moreover, it was the New Right's agenda, rather than traditional Republican concerns with judicial self-restraint, that defined the Reagan administration's approach to judicial selection. Nothing symbolized that more than Meese's call for a "return to a jurisprudence of original intention," and Judge Robert H. Bork's defense of that position during his ill-fated confirmation hearing on his nomination to the Court in 1987 (Bork 1990; Meese 1985, 701–704). Beyond stirring a jurisprudential debate, it meant appointing judges who would limit the federal government and return power to the states over a range of issues—abortion, education, school prayer, free speech, and criminal justice.

During eight years in the Oval Office, Reagan transformed the politics of judicial appointments and changed the composition of the federal bench. He appointed close to half of all federal judges and, along with elevating Rehnquist to the chief justiceship, appointed three other justices: Sandra Day O'Connor in 1981, Antonin Scalia in 1986, and Anthony Kennedy in 1988. Numbers are only part of the story, though. No less importantly, the Reagan administration's rigorous screening process for judicial nominees led it to draw the line on simply rewarding party faithful and to reject potential nominees advanced by moderate Republicans in favor of more controversial conservatives. Such a screening process sharply polarized the judicial appointment process, resulting in some intra-party fighting within Republican ranks over lower court judges, which badly divided the Republican legal establishment and ultimately contributed to the defeat of Bork's nomination to the Court (O'Brien 1988).

Admittedly, Reagan's successor gave less priority to federal judges (Goldman 1993; Carp, et al. 1993), and Bush's two appointees to the Court are a "mixed bag": Justice David H. Souter after a few terms became aligned with other left-of-center justices, whereas Justice Clarence Thomas sides with the chief justice and Reagan's three other appointees to form a bare majority willing to reconsider basic tenets of the post–New Deal jurisprudence and to curb congressional power (O'Brien 1996).

Still, the fact remains that Reagan and Bush tipped the balance on the Court and sharply polarized the process of judicial appointments in naming to the federal bench a large number of conservatives identified with the New Right. Notably, a number of their lower court judges, like Judges Wilkinson and Michael J. Luttig, among others, clerked at the Court and then went to work in the Reagan and Bush administrations before their judicial appointments; they later became known for sending their clerks on to work in the Rehnquist Court. By the 1990s, movement conservatives were also well established with organizations like the Federalist Society, Free Congress Foundation, and the Washington Legal Foundation, monitoring judicial selection and dedicated to preserving the Reagan/Bush judicial legacy by opposing Clinton's judicial nominees.

Remarkably, after twelve years of Republican-picked judges and how polarized the judicial selection process had become, in his first couple of years Clinton paid little attention to judgeships. He was slow to make nominations and either sought to avoid controversial nominees or abandoned those targeted by conservatives. Hence, he avoided bitter confirmation battles by naming two moderate nominees to the Court: Justices Ruth Bader Ginsburg and Stephen Breyer. Subsequently, his administration became institutionally constrained after the 1994 midterm elections compounded his problems with a divided government, and in particular a Republican-controlled Senate. In his second term, Republicans increasingly delayed confirmation hearings on judicial nominees and forced Clinton to abandon some nominees and to name conservatives picked by Republican senators in exchange for the Senate's voting on confirmations (O'Brien 2000d).

In sum, the politics of judicial appointments was transformed in the 1980s and 1990s. The politics of rewarding party faithful and institutional accommodation between the White House and the Senate gave way to a more intensely ideological and conservative interest-group driven politics of appointing federal judges. That was perhaps inevitable since the political parties also became weaker, while congressional districts became increasingly homogeneous in partisan terms, and Congress became more politically polarized (Green and Shea 1999; Sinclair 1997; Sinclair 1995; Rohde 1991; Jacobson 1991). In any event, those forces exacerbated the tensions between Congress and the president, and changed the composition and direction of the federal judiciary.

THE REHNQUIST COURT'S JUDICIAL ACTIVISM

It is often misleading to refer to a period of the Court's history in terms of the presiding chief justice. The chief justice is, after all, only the first among equals and rarely does the body of the Court's work bear the imprint of the chief justice's jurisprudence. Thus, "the Burger Court" is a misnomer (Blasi 1983; Schwartz 1983, arguing that the Warren Court was in fact the Brennan Court; Tushnet 1993, arguing that the Warren Court as a cultural phenomenon persisted into the Burger Court years). Yet, arguably, that is not so with "the Rehnquist Court," at least in the 1990s, because large bodies of constitutional law have moved in the direction of Chief Justice Rehnquist's well-staked-out positions (O'Brien 1987).

Chief Justice Rehnquist has been called "the Compleat Jeffersonian" because of his long-standing opposition to the expansion of the federal government and defense of the interests of states (Davis 1989; Powell 1982; Shapiro 1976). As a law clerk at the Court in the early 1950s he opposed the Court's eventual ruling in the landmark school desegregation decision in *Brown v. Board of Education* (1954) (O'Brien 2000c). As an Arizona attorney and political activist in the 1960s, he opposed passage of public accommodation laws. In the 1970s and early 1980s as an associate justice he earned the nickname "Lone Ranger" for filing so many solo dissenting opinions, frequently championing federalism concerns.

Chief Justice Rehnquist embodies and symbolizes (which is why in 1986 Reagan elevated him to the center chair) the forces redrawing the constitutional boundaries between the national government and the states, along with congressional–judicial relations. Admittedly, Chief Justice Rehnquist has not always prevailed: a plurality of the Court, for instance, declined to overrule *Roe v. Wade* (1973) and *Planned Parenthood of Southeastern Pennsylvania v. Casey* (1992), and extended the Fourteenth Amendment equal protection guarantee to gays and lesbians (*Romer v. Evans* 1996). Still, Chief Justice Rehnquist's views have generally prevailed in wide areas of criminal law—ranging from rulings on unreasonable searches and seizures (O'Brien 2000c, 859–870), to the imposition of capital punishment and expediting executions (O'Brien 2000c, 1115–1125). He also commanded a majority for ending federal court–ordered efforts to achieve integrated schools and for returning control to local school boards (*Freeman v. Pitts* 1992). In these and other areas, judicial supervision of state and local policies has been significantly curbed. At the same time, though, a majority of the Rehnquist Court has been willing to thwart the democratic process and assert judicial power in striking down local, state, and federal affirmative-action programs (*City of Richmond v. J.A. Croson* 1989; *Adarand Constructors v. Pena* 1995), as well as the creation of minority–majority voting districts (*Shaw v. Reno* 1993).

The center piece—perhaps, as Judge Wilkinson contends, the major legacy—of the Rehnquist Court is unmistakably its defense of "states' sovereignty" in relation to congressional power. As with rulings invalidating affirmative-action programs, the chief justice usually commands only a bare majority. Moreover, he does so not primarily due to his persuasive powers but rather because of how the Court's composition changed in the late 1980s and early 1990s with the appointments of Reagan and Bush justices. For example, Rehnquist was able to form a bare majority for resurrecting the Tenth Amendment in defense of the "states *qua* states" and, for the first time since before the 1937 New Deal crisis, limit congressional power in the 1976 decision of *National League of Cities v. Usery* (overturning *Maryland v. Wirtz* 1968). *Usery* struck down three 1974 amendments to the Fair Labor Standards Act of 1938, one of the last major pieces of New Deal legislation, that extended minimum-wage and maximum-hour standards to state and local employees. Yet, almost a decade later, *Usery* was overturned in *Garcia v. San Antonio Metropolitan Transit Authority* (1985), upholding the application of federal minimum-wage and overtime standards to local employees. And in spite of Chief Justice Rehnquist's bare majority for limiting Congress's power in the 1990s, *Garcia* has not been overruled, although the Court was invited to do so (*New York v. United States* 1992).

Although Chief Justice Rehnquist's bare majority has been unable to articulate a clear and workable Tenth Amendment principle, and has been forced to rely instead on arguments drawn from the "history and structure" of federalism, it obviously no longer shares the position advanced by *Garcia*'s bare majority, namely, that the Court should exercise self-restraint and defer to the national political process—specifically, Congress—to determine the boundaries between the national government and the states (O'Brien 1989b).

The turning point came in 1992 with *New York v. United States*.[1] There, although declining to overturn *Garcia* and conceding that the Tenth Amendment "is essentially a tautology," Justice O'Connor ruled that Congress exceeded its power under Article I in requiring states that failed to provide disposal sites for low-level radioactive waste to "take-title" and to assume liability for all undisposed waste. Congress, according to the Rehnquist's bare majority, may not command the states to enact a law or perform a function in order to implement a federal regulation. In other words, Congress may use the proverbial "carrot" of conditioning states' receipt of federal funds in order to get them to adopt laws or implement policies, such as raising the minimum drinking age (*South Dakota v. Dole* 1987), but Congress may not use the "stick" of directing state governments to do so under Article I.

Subsequently, a bare majority of the Rehnquist Court further curbed congressional power under Article I in *United States v. Lopez* (1995). Writing for the Court, Chief Justice Rehnquist struck down provisions of the Gun-Free School Zones Act of 1990, which made it a federal crime to possess a firearm within 1,000 feet of a school, because Congress failed to show (and a bare majority of the Court was unwilling to find) that gun violence in schools "substantially affects commerce." Two years later, in *Printz v. United States* (1997) and *Mack v. United States* (1997), in two more five-to-four decisions, the Court invalidated provisions of the Brady Handgun Violence Prevention Act of 1993 that had temporarily required state and local law enforcement officials to conduct background checks on handgun purchasers. Once again, the Rehnquist Court reaffirmed that Congress "may not compel the States to enact or administer a federal regulatory program." And *Lopez*'s bare majority extended its analysis, in *United States v. Morrison* (2000), in striking down the Violence Against Women Act of 1994.

Besides these rulings on "inherent limitations" of congressional power under Article I, a bare majority of the Rehnquist Court resurrected the Eleventh Amendment guarantee for states' sovereign immunity from lawsuits filed in federal courts by citizens of other states or countries, and expanded its scope as a further limitation on congressional power. In *Seminole Tribe of Florida v. Florida* (1996), Chief Justice Rehnquist again commanded a bare majority in striking down a provision in the Indian Gaming Regulatory Act of 1988 that authorized tribes to sue states in federal courts if they failed to negotiate gaming compacts. Congressional authorization for tribes to sue states in federal court, over another bitter dissent by Justices Stevens, Souter, Ginsburg, and Breyer, was deemed to abrogate states' sovereign immunity.

Seminole Tribe was then extended (*Florida Prepaid Postsecondary Education Expense Board v. College Savings Bank* [1999], most notably in *Alden v. Maine* (1999) and the following year in *Kimel v. Florida Board of Regents* (2000). *Alden* held that the Eleventh Amendment and the Constitution's "structure and history" of federalism renders states immune from lawsuits filed in *state* courts by state and local employees seeking to enforce federal standards for overtime pay. *Kimel* held that state employees could not sue state and local governments in *federal* courts in order to force their compliance with the federal Age Discrimination in Employment Act. Likewise, *Vermont Agency of Natural Resources v. United States ex rel. Stevens* (2000) held that private citizens may not sue states in federal courts to enforce provisions of the False Claims Act. In short, while Congress may extend federal employment standards to state and local employees, under *Garcia*, those employees cannot sue in either state or federal courts to force states' compliance with federal law.

In addition, the Rehnquist Court has limited Congress's lawmaking authority under section 5 of the Fourteenth Amendment. In the Religious Freedom Restoration Act of 1993, Congress sought to reestablish in federal law a standard that the Court had jettisoned, in *Oregon v. Smith* (1990), for balancing claims to religious freedom against governmental interests in otherwise generally applicable laws. But when the constitutionality of that law was challenged in *City of Boerne v. Flores* (1997) the Court ruled that Congress exceeded its enforcement power under section 5 and lacks "the power to determine what constitutes a constitutional violation." That limitation on congressional power was reaffirmed in *Kimel v. Florida Board of Regents*, invalidating provisions of the Age Discrimination in Employment Act as applied to state and local governments. In these and other rulings, the Rehnquist Court underscored its power over Congress in defining the scope of constitutional rights and governmental powers.[2]

CONCLUSION

How significant is the Rehnquist Court's redefinition of Congress's lawmaking authority versus that of the states and of congressional–judicial relations? Court watchers and legal scholars are, frankly, divided (Derthick 2000; Tushnet 1999; Choper 1998; Fried 1995).

On the one hand, Congress still has extensive lawmaking authority under Article I, at least as long as the regulated activity "substantially affects commerce." The Court also distinguished *New York* and *Printz* in *Reno v. Condon* (2000) when upholding the Drivers Privacy Protection Act of 1994, that regulates the disclosure of personal information contained in records of state motor vehicles departments. The Rehnquist Court also continues to enforce its dormant commerce clause jurisprudence in striking down state laws that interfere with the national free-market economy, even though Congress has not asserted its power under Article I (O'Brien 1993). And in *United States v. Locke* (2000), the Court unanimously struck down state environmental and navigational regulations that were more stringent than federal standards and those mandated in international agreements and treaties. Likewise in *Crosby v. National Foreign Trade Council* (2000) the Court unanimously struck down Massachusetts's restrictions on businesses doing business with Myanmar (Burma), as an interference with Congress's power over foreign commerce. Moreover, as noted earlier, Congress remains free to provide incentives for, or condition the receipt of federal funds upon, states' compliance with federal law and policies.

On the other hand, though, a bare majority of the Rehnquist Court has clearly made it more difficult for Congress to expand federal criminal law. The Eleventh Amendment has also emerged as a barrier to litigation aimed at forcing state and local governments' compliance with federal standards. And congressional power under section 5 of the Fourteenth Amendment has been curbed as well.

In historical and political perspective, the tensions in congressional–judicial relations have not reached the red-hot level of 1937. But, by comparison with the judicial deference accorded Congress for almost a half century after the 1937 "constitutional crisis," a bare majority of the Rehnquist Court is unquestionably much less deferential to Congress and to the national political process.

How much farther the Rehnquist Court goes in curtailing congressional power remains to unfold. In the meantime, it appears fair to conclude that the Rehnquist Court has significantly altered congressional–judicial relations as a result of its judicial activism and lack of deference to Congress in redrawing the boundaries between federal and state lawmaking powers. And that in turn may further intensify the sharply polarized politics of federal judicial appointments that produced the Rehnquist Court in the first place.

NOTES

1. In addition, in *Gregory v. Ashcroft*, 501 U.S. 452 (1991), the Court adopted a rule requiring Congress to make a "plain statement" that it intends to preempt state laws; otherwise the Court will presume that states have not been preempted.

2. See also *Clinton v. City of New York*, 118 S.Ct. 2091 (1998) (invalidating the Line Item Veto Act of 1995); and *Florida Prepaid Postsecondary Education Expense Board v. College Savings Bank*, 119 S.Ct. 2199 (1999) (holding that Congress had not shown that violations of federal patent rights by states were serious enough to justify Congress's using section 5 of the Fourteenth Amendment to create a remedy for such violations).

CHAPTER SIX

Congress, the Court, and Religious Liberty: The Case of *Employment Division of Oregon v. Smith*

CAROLYN N. LONG

For the last decade Congress and the Court have been engaged in a heated conversation about the appropriate level of protection that should be afforded to religious liberty under the free exercise guarantee of the First Amendment to the Constitution. Congress's role as one of many constitutional interpreters is not unique. In chapter two of this book Louis Fisher provides a number of historical examples of Congress acting as a coordinate branch of government to give meaning to the Constitution and to act as a check on the other branches of government. In the area of religious liberty, Congress has been particularly vigilant in its efforts to circumvent Supreme Court decisions it finds disagreeable. In 1987 Congress enacted legislation to allow members of the armed forces to wear religious apparel after the Court refused to protect this right under the free exercise clause of the First Amendment, and the following year Congress enacted legislation allowing religious exemptions from the payment of social security taxes, which the Court previously determined was not warranted under the Constitution. In each instance lawmakers essentially told the Court that they disagreed with its interpretation of the level of protection provided to religious exercise under the Constitution, and then used their authority to enact federal legislation that provides greater protection for religious liberty.

This chapter takes a closer look at Congress's role as a constitutional interpreter by taking a detailed look at the colloquy between Congress and the Court on the issue of religious liberty. The conversation begins with the Court's 1990 decision, *Employment Division of Oregon v. Smith* where it refused to protect the sacramental use of peyote under the First Amendment, and in the process also removed an entire category of laws—neutral and generally applicable laws that

significantly burden one's religious exercise—from protection under the
Constitution. Congress then enters into the conversation by using its enforcement authority under the Fourteenth Amendment to enact the Religious
Freedom Restoration Act (RFRA), which reinstated the application of the compelling government interest test in cases where a neutral and generally federal,
state, or local law substantially burdens religious exercise. Congress also responds
with an amendment to the American Indian Religious Freedom Act of 1978 to
exempt the sacramental use of peyote, the central issue in *Smith* (1990), from
federal and state controlled-substances laws. The Court then answers Congress
by using its power of judicial review to strike down RFRA as a violation of states'
rights, and in the process, reminds Congress that it also violated the principle of
separation of powers because interpretation of the Constitution must take place
on the Court's, not Congress's, terms. Congress, ever vigilant, confronts the
Court once again with introduction of the Religious Liberty Protection Act
(RLPA), which would protect religious exercise in the same manner as RFRA,
but which relies on Congress's Article I power over spending and commerce.
Although RLPA has yet to be enacted into law, it is important to note that
Congress's consideration of this legislation is being framed, in part, by its understanding that a slim majority on the Rehnquist Court has recently handed down
a series of decisions that curbs congressional power in defense of states' sovereignty. After reviewing this constitutional conversation, this chapter ends with
some thoughts on the advantages of having Congress engage in a constitutional
dialogue with the Court.

EMPLOYMENT DIVISION OF OREGON V. SMITH

In 1983 Alfred Smith, a Klamath Indian, and Galen Black, a non-Indian, were
terminated from their jobs as drug and alcohol treatment counselors for the
Douglas County Council on Alcohol and Drug Abuse Prevention and Treatment
(ADAPT) for ingesting peyote, a hallucinogenic substance, at a religious ceremony of the Native American Church (*Smith v. Employment Division* [1986]).[1]
The private drug and alcohol treatment facility fired the men for misconduct for
intentionally violating its strict zero-tolerance drug and alcohol policy.[2] Prior to
their use of peyote, which is listed as a Schedule I drug under Oregon state law,
both Smith and Black were warned that use of the substance, even as part of a
religious ceremony, could result in termination from their jobs. Nevertheless, on
separate occasions, they knowingly and voluntarily ingested the sacrament at a
church ceremony. After their termination from ADAPT, Smith and Black
applied for unemployment benefits from the state of Oregon, which were denied
by the Department of Human Resources, because under Oregon law, individuals dismissed for misconduct are not entitled to unemployment benefits.[3] The

benefits were briefly reinstated after an independent review of the denial of compensation, but the Employment Appeals Board (EAB) later reversed this action.

Smith and Black appealed the denial of compensation to the Oregon court of appeals, which reversed the EAB decision and reinstated the unemployment benefits (*Smith v. Employment Division* [Or. Ct. App. 1985]). The Oregon Supreme Court upheld the decision, ruled that the claimants' use of peyote was a religious act, and stated that the denial of unemployment benefits upon release from the rehabilitation center constituted a burden upon the claimants' right to freely exercise their religion under the First Amendment. In its evaluation of the First Amendment free exercise challenge, the state supreme court applied the highest level of judicial scrutiny, the compelling government interest balancing test, used for almost three decades in federal free exercise clause cases since the U.S. Supreme Court's decision in *Sherbert v. Verner* (1963), to issue the religious liberty challenge that, "the person claiming the free exercise right must show the application of the law in question significantly burdens the free exercise of his religion." If the person shows this burden, the state then must demonstrate that the constraint on the religious activity is the least restrictive means of achieving a " 'compelling' state interest" (*Smith* 1986, 217). The Court determined that the state's denial of unemployment benefits placed a burden on the claimants' ability to exercise their religion, and that the state's interest in uniformly applying the law and preserving the financial integrity of the unemployment compensation fund were not compelling enough to deny compensation. The Oregon Supreme Court rejected the Board's contention that the legality of peyote in the state was a factor to be considered in the case (*Smith* 1986, 210).[4]

The Employment Division for the state of Oregon appealed the decision to the U.S. Supreme Court, which handed down its decision vacating the ruling and remanding the case back to Oregon (*Employment Division of Oregon v. Smith* [1988]). The Court disagreed with the Oregon court's conclusion that the illegality of peyote was not constitutionally relevant. Writing for the majority, Justice Stevens, joined by Chief Justice Rehnquist and Justices White, O'Connor, and Scalia, stated: "For if a State has prohibited through its criminal laws certain kinds of religiously motivated conduct without violating the First Amendment, it certainly follows that it may impose the lesser burden of denying unemployment compensation benefits to persons who engage in that conduct" (*Smith* 1988, 670). He noted that in precedent cases where an employee was required to choose between fidelity to religious beliefs or acceptance of unemployment benefits and the Court ruled in favor of the religious claimants, that "[t]he results we reached . . . might well have been different if the employees had been discharged for engaging in criminal conduct" (*Smith* 1988, 670). Stevens explained that the First Amendment free exercise clause protected only "legitimate" claims to the free exercise of religion, not conduct that the state has forbidden through its criminal statutes (*Smith* 1988, 671). However, because the Court was unable to determine from the record whether the sacramental use of peyote was against the law, it sent the case back to the Oregon Supreme Court to decide this issue.

On remand, the state court ruled that the criminal prohibition of peyote extended to religious as well as recreational use of the peyote, which made Smith and Black guilty of violating the law, but it reiterated that this prohibition against the sacramental use of peyote violated the free exercise clause of the federal Constitution. It therefore reaffirmed its earlier holding that the state's denial of unemployment benefits violated the claimants' religious freedom guaranteed under the First Amendment (*Smith v. Employment Division of Oregon* 1988, 72–73).

The state of Oregon once again appealed the case to the U.S. Supreme Court, which reversed the state court ruling, and, in the process, established a new constitutional standard for free exercise cases (*Employment Division of Oregon v. Smith* [1990]). The decision is notable more for its rejection of what many believed was a traditional understanding of the protection provided to religious claimants under the free exercise clause of the First Amendment than for the result of the immediate case at hand (Day 1991; Gordon 1991; Marin 1991; Laycock 1993; Rawlings 1995; Titus 1995). Justice Scalia wrote the majority opinion, joined by Chief Justice Rehnquist and Justices White, Stevens, and Kennedy. He determined that while the free exercise clause of the First Amendment absolutely protected freedom of religious beliefs, it did not protect all forms of religious conduct. The free exercise clause, he explained, only protected religious action when the state has acted in an intentional manner that was "specifically directed" at religiously inspired behavior (*Smith* 1990, 878). According to his reading of previous free exercise jurisprudence, the Court had "never held that an individual's religious beliefs excuse him from compliance with an otherwise valid law prohibiting conduct that the State is free to regulate" (*Smith* 1990, 878–89). To support this contention, Scalia selectively cited precedent that supported his argument and explained away others that presented a contrary view.[5] He then announced that in cases where the burden placed on one's religion was the result of the neutral application of a generally applicable law, that it was only necessary that the action fulfill the rational basis test, the lowest level of judicial scrutiny. If there is a rational basis for a law, then the free exercise clause cannot be used as a defense. Justice Scalia explicitly rejected the use of the compelling government interest test in these instances, despite the fact that the standard had been used fairly consistently in federal free exercise cases since the *Sherbert* decision.[6]

According to Scalia, use of a high level of judicial scrutiny in all free exercise cases would make every person "a law unto himself" and "any society adopting such a system would be courting anarchy" (*Smith* 1990, 888). He suggested that religious proponents instead resort to the political process for the protection of their religious practices. In his evaluation of the case before the Court, Scalia ruled that because the respondents ingested a substance that was illegal under a valid, generally applicable criminal law, the state could, "consistent with the free exercise clause, deny the respondents unemployment compensation when their dismissal results from use of the drug" (*Smith* 1990, 890).

Employment Division v. Smith stunned individuals in the religious and civil liberties communities, not to mention many constitutional law scholars, who had expected, at worst, a decision denying the respondents' request for unemployment compensation. Instead, the Supreme Court reached beyond the case to remove an entire category of laws outside the protection of the free exercise clause. The decision, which had not received much media attention up to this point, was widely denounced in the popular press and in academic and legal journals. As well-known constitutional scholar William Bentley Ball recognized, "What first appeared to be a trivial free exercise challenge to an unemployment compensation ruling has resulted in a constitutional fault of San Andreas proportions" (Day 1991). Criticism focused upon the Court's misreading of free exercise precedent, its judicial activism for reinventing the Court's free exercise jurisprudence, and its suggestion that religious adherents resort to the political process to request exemptions from neutral, generally applicable laws that burdened religious beliefs. It was this latter suggestion that prompted some to think about how to respond to the Supreme Court. Could Congress use the political process to circumvent the Court's ruling in *Smith*?

THE RELIGIOUS FREEDOM RESTORATION ACT

Within days after the Court's ruling, the Coalition for the Free Exercise of Religion, an eclectic alliance of religious and civil liberties organizations, united together in opposition to *Smith*. Members of the coalition represented both sides of the ideological spectrum, from groups on the left such as the American Civil Liberties Union and the Baptist Joint Committee on Public Affairs, to groups on the right, such as the National Association for Evangelicals and the Christian Legal Society. The coalition quickly decided that the best way to address the problem created by the decision was to have Congress enact legislation that would reinstate the compelling government interest test in cases where a neutral, generally applicable law placed a substantial burden on an individual's free exercise of religion. This high level of scrutiny would better protect religious exercise than the lower rationality review announced in *Smith*.

The coalition approached Representative Stephen Solarz (D-N.Y.) to lead the legislative effort. The choice of Solarz was no accident; he had previously been involved in congressional efforts to respond to Supreme Court decisions that restricted religious freedom. Most notably, Solarz led the fight for passage of legislation that allows members of the armed forces to wear neat and conservative religious apparel while in uniform unless it interfered with the performance of military duties. Public Law 100-180 was enacted in direct response to the Supreme Court's 1986 *Goldman v. Weinberger* (1986, 510) decision where a five-member majority determined that free exercise challenges in the military context were of such a "special circumstance" that the Court should defer to the judgment of military authorities and use the more deferential rationality review to evaluate free exercise challenges in this context.[7] To some observers, the Court's decision in *Goldman* was a predecessor to *Smith*, where it abandoned application of the compelling government interest test altogether in cases where government has not acted directly to burden religion.

Attention to a legislative correction of *Smith* initially focused on whether Congress had the constitutional authority to respond to the decision. Members of the coalition worked with Solarz to craft an argument that Congress had the power under section 5 of the Fourteenth Amendment, which grants Congress the "power to enforce, by appropriate legislation, the provisions of this article," to independently secure constitutional rights, including the protection of the free exercise of religion (Choper 1982; Carter 1986; McConnell 1991; McConnell 1995; Laycock 1995). Congress had previously used its section 5 authority to enact federal anti-discrimination legislation such as the 1964 and 1990 civil rights acts and the 1965 Voting Rights Act. Each law provides statutory protection for civil rights and liberties beyond what is required by the Supreme Court. And because the due process clause of the Fourteenth Amendment makes the free exercise clause, as well as other guarantees of the Bill of Rights, binding against encroachments by states, this section 5 authority empowers Congress to protect the free exercise of religion.

The Supreme Court previously recognized Congress's section 5 authority to remedy state violations of Fourteenth Amendment rights. In *Katzenbach v. Morgan* (1966), a case involving a challenge to the 1965 Voting Rights Act, the Court sustained a portion of the bill that provided that states could not deny individuals who completed the sixth grade in an accredited Spanish-language school in Puerto Rico the right to vote. Congress enacted the law, in part, to ensure nondiscrimination in voting. It was challenged by a group in New York that was defending a state law that required English literacy as a prerequisite to voting rights—a law the Supreme Court sustained as legitimate. *Morgan* established the precedent that Congress could act independently of the Court to protect rights and liberties against violations by state and local governments as long as it did not "restrict, abrogate, or dilute" the protections in the Bill of Rights (*Morgan* 1966, 651 n. 10). To some, the decision also appeared to grant

Congress the power to define the substantive scope of constitutional guarantees. Subsequent Supreme Court decisions on this issue reaffirmed Congress's authority to enact legislation pursuant to its section 5 authority under the Fourteenth Amendment, as well as congressional power to act in a similar fashion under the enforcement clauses of the Thirteenth and Fifteenth amendments.[8] The line of decisions unquestionably established Congress's right to use its enforcement authority to adopt remedial and preventative legislation to protect constitutional rights against abuses by state and local governments. However, Congress's right to modify the Court's substantive constitutional interpretations was less than clear. Despite this uncertainty, key members of the Coalition for the Free Exercise of Religion believed it was appropriate for Congress to use its section 5 enforcement authority as an avenue to address *Smith*.

The coalition's legislative drafting committee worked with constitutional law scholars and members of Solarz's staff on this legislative response, and three months later introduced the Religious Freedom Restoration Act to Congress. The act mandated the use of the compelling government interest test to religious challenges to any federal, state, or local law that significantly burdened religious exercise. The measure would not directly overturn the Court's constitutional ruling in *Smith*—its free exercise analysis would still stand—rather it would circumvent the decision by creating a judicially enforceable statute that protected religious freedom. The legislation was presented as a statutory solution to the Court's unwillingness to provide a high level of protection for religious exercise. The act reflected its sponsors' belief that religious liberty should be protected to the highest extent and subject to restriction for only the most compelling reasons. Technically, the *Smith* rule would continue to govern free exercise challenges brought under the First Amendment; however, RFRA would provide religious adherents a more sympathetic forum for challenges to government regulations that interfered with religious practices. Significantly, RFRA would leave the determination of whether or not an exemption to a government regulation should be granted to the courts, which would then balance the state's interest in the law against the burden on the religious adherent. Thus, the measure has been described as performing a constitutional function because it creates "a statutory right where the Supreme Court declined to create a constitutional right" (Laycock 1993).

The initial hearing on RFRA in the House Subcommittee on Civil and Constitutional Rights reflected heated criticism of *Smith* and strong bipartisan support for the measure. It is clear from the committee record that Congress was motivated to enact the legislation because it believed the Supreme Court had erred in its interpretation of the free exercise clause in *Smith*, which left an individual's religious exercise unprotected against infringements from neutral, generally applicable laws. The intention of the act, as stated in the "purposes" section of the measure, was to restore free exercise law to the status that existed prior to *Smith*, when the Court applied the compelling government interest test to most religious liberty challenges. Representative Solarz, who appeared on behalf of the legislation, described it as a "narrowly crafted, legislative response to the radical work of an activist Supreme Court majority" (House Subcommittee on Civil and Constitutional Rights 1990, 18). Witnesses appearing before the subcommittee stressed the need for Congress to correct "mistakes" by the Court, and predicted that an increasingly conservative Supreme Court would lead Americans to future appeals to Congress for the protection of rights and liberties (House Subcommittee on Civil and Constitutional Rights 1990, 17).

The Religious Freedom Restoration Act died in committee as the 101st Congress (1989–1990) came to a close, but was reintroduced the next year. However, in the interim between sessions, the bipartisan support in favor of the bill began to show signs of eroding as several pro-life groups, led by the U.S. Catholic League and the National Right to Life Committee, voiced their opposition to the measure because of their concern that RFRA would create a religious right to abortion and would negatively affect the tax-exempt status and public funding for religious organizations. The second round of congressional hearings in the 102nd Congress (1991–92) reflected these concerns, as well as differing opinions over whether the Religious Freedom Restoration Act was unconstitutional because it infringed upon state sovereignty (House Subcommittee on Civil and Constitutional Rights 1992; Senate Committee on the Judiciary 1992). The measure once again died in committee at the end of the session. However, by the time RFRA was introduced for a third time in the 103rd Congress (1993–94), these issues were resolved and the bill was reported favorably out of the House and Senate judiciary committees. The measure was briefly held up in the Senate over the issue of how the measure would affect prisoners' religious claims, but it finally passed both houses of Congress with overwhelmingly bipartisan support and was signed into law by President Clinton on November 16, 1993 (Public Law 102-141 codified at 42 U.S.C. § 2000bb).

AMENDMENTS TO THE AMERICAN INDIAN RELIGIOUS FREEDOM ACT

At the same time the Coalition for the Free Exercise of Religion was working on behalf of congressional efforts to enact RFRA, another equally diverse umbrella group, the American Indian Religious Freedom Coalition (AIRFC), was working with members of Congress to enact outcome-specific legislation to safeguard Indian religious practices. The coalition, made up of Indian rights organizations and religious, civil, and environmental rights groups, formed soon after the Supreme Court's decision in *Lyng v. Northwest Cemetery Association* (1989). In *Lyng* a sharply divided Court determined that the building of a road through land considered sacred by three American Indian tribes did not constitute a burden on the tribes' exercise of religion because it did not "coerce" them to act against their religious beliefs. The Court therefore declined to apply the compelling government interest test to the dispute because the burden threshold had not been fulfilled, and used rationality review instead to deny the religious liberty claim. When *Smith* was decided, the coalition also focused its attention on the need for federal legislation to specifically protect the religious use of peyote. At the time of the decision, twenty-two states had no legislative protection for the non-drug use of the sacrament. The laws in the twenty-eight states that did offer legislative protection provided varying degrees of coverage from a total religious exemption to controlled-substances laws for all individuals practicing peyotism, to the limited protection of an "affirmative defense" for individuals convicted of violating a state criminal law proscribing possession or use of peyote.

In 1990 and 1991 the American Indian Religious Freedom Coalition held several "Religious Freedom Summits" where resolutions were drafted criticizing the Supreme Court for its anti-Indian decisions. Appeals were made to Congress to correct *Smith* and *Lyng*. Later, AIRFC worked with representatives and senators to arrange field hearings to highlight the need to protect American Indian religious freedom. In the Senate the coalition worked primarily with Senator Daniel Inouye, a Democrat from Hawaii, who previously championed legislative efforts to protect Indian religious freedom, including sponsorship of the 1990 Native American Grave Protection and Repatriation Act, and in the House, the coalition reached out to then-Representative Bill Richardson (D-N.Mex.). The hearings, held in 1992 and 1993, resulted in a consensus on the need for federal legislation to preserve sacred Indian sites, protection for the religious use of peyote, increased access to sacred objects, particularly eagle feathers and parts, and protection for religious rights of Native American prisoners.

In 1993 Senator Inouye introduced the Native American Free Exercise of Religion Act in the Senate, and the next year similar legislation was introduced in the House. The measures reflected the consensus that came from Indian communities after the 1992 and 1993 field hearings: federal protection for sacred Indian sites, the sacramental use of peyote, access to sacred Indian objects, and the religious rights of incarcerated American Indians. Like RFRA, the measures ran into some problems as they were deliberated in Congress, particularly from several witnesses who questioned the constitutionality of the legislation, and from interest groups representing the forestry and mining industries that opposed the provision protecting sacred sites. By the end of 1994 it was necessary to divide the Native American Free Exercise of Religion Act into two separate bills; one to protect the sacramental use of peyote, and the second to protect access to sacred Indian sites and the religious rights of incarcerated American Indians. The peyote bill eventually passed both houses of Congress with strong bipartisan support, and was signed into law by President Clinton on October 6, 1994 (Public Law 103-344 codified at 42 U.S.C. 1996). The legislation adds a new section to the American Indian Religious Freedom Act of 1978; it exempts the religious use of peyote in bona fide traditional ceremonies from state and federal controlled-substances laws and prohibits discrimination for the use of peyote. The second bill died in Congress at the end of the session, and has not been seriously considered since.

However, action by the executive branch addressed some of these issues. In April of 1994 President Clinton issued an executive memorandum to the heads of all executive departments and agencies asking for simplification of the process for the collection and transfer of eagle parts for Indian religious purposes. The memorandum also requested that the Department of the Interior streamline the process of working with Indian tribes on access to sacred eagle parts and feathers.[9] And in March 1996, President Clinton signed an executive order to promote the preservation of sacred Indian sites (Executive Order 13007). Clinton's efforts on behalf of Indian religious freedom is significant in its own right; it serves as an example of a president acting in his capacity as the head of a coordinate branch of government to also enter into this conversation about the need to protect religious liberty in America.

CITY OF BOERNE V. FLORES

Several weeks after Congress enacted the Religious Freedom Restoration Act, P. F. Flores, the archbishop of San Antonio, became involved in a zoning dispute with the city of Boerne, Texas, which set into motion another confrontation between Congress and the Court. The case involved the city council's denial of Flores's request for a building permit to renovate and expand the Saint Peter Catholic Church, which was located in a district protected by a historic landmark preservation ordinance. Flores filed suit in the U.S. District Court for Western Texas under the Religious Freedom Restoration Act, charging that the permit denial placed a substantial burden on his parish's ability to freely exercise its religion. The city defended the denial as reasonable, and answered the RFRA challenge by arguing that the statute was unconstitutional. The District Court for Western Texas agreed, ruling that the legislation was facially invalid because it infringed upon the "long-settled authority of the courts . . . to say what the law is," thus violating the principle in *Marbury v. Madison* (1803) that the judiciary has the ultimate authority to interpret the Constitution (*Flores v. City of Boerne* [1995]). The court also ruled that Congress had not appropriately invoked its power under section 5 of the Fourteenth Amendment when it enacted the legislation. Flores appealed the ruling to the Fifth Circuit, which reversed it in a unanimous decision, noting that Congress had acted appropriately under its enforcement authority under the Fourteenth Amendment, and that the legislation did not violate the principle of separation of powers because the executive and legislative branches of government have a "right and duty to interpret the constitution" and to assign a "higher value to free exercise of secured freedoms than the value assigned by the Courts" (*Flores v. City of Boerne* 1996). The city of Boerne appealed the decision to the U.S. Supreme Court, which agreed to hear the case, giving it the opportunity to decide on the constitutionality of the legislation Congress had enacted in response to *Smith*.

On June 25, 1997, the Court handed down its decision in *Boerne v. Flores* (1997), ruling that the Religious Freedom Restoration Act unconstitutionally violated the principles of federalism and separation of powers. It was a busy week for the Court; over the next two days it also struck down the Communications Decency Act in *Reno v. ACLU* (1997) and a section of the 1993 Brady Handgun Violence Prevention Act in *Printz v. United States* (1997). Moreover, in both *Boerne* and *Printz* the Court specifically rejected an expansive interpretation of congressional power, finding instead that Congress had encroached upon states' rights.

Justice Kennedy wrote the majority opinion, joined by Chief Justice Rehnquist and Justices Scalia, Thomas, Stevens, and Ginsberg. He determined that Congress exceeded its authority when it enacted RFRA because it attempted to substantively define the free exercise clause, which was inappropriate under section 5 of the Fourteenth Amendment, which only empowered Congress to enact "remedial" or "preventative" legislation that enforced that amendment's guarantee of civil rights. Interpretation of constitutional rights, which RFRA attempts to do, stated Kennedy, was a power reserved for the judiciary. He noted, "[l]egislation which alters the meaning of the free exercise clause cannot be said to be enforcing the clause. Congress does not enforce a constitutional right by changing what the right is. It has been given the power 'to enforce,' not the power to determine what constitutes a constitutional violation" (*Boerne* 1997, 519). The responsibility of defining constitutional rights, Kennedy continued, was the province of the judiciary. He then cited *Marbury* to reiterate the Court's conclusion that it alone has supremacy over the interpretation of the Constitution.

Kennedy also differentiated RFRA from the Voting Rights Act, which RFRA proponents had argued was similar in form. The Voting Rights Act, he noted, was classified as "remedial" legislation because Congress had a factual basis to determine "invidious discrimination in violation of the equal protection clause" (*Boerne* 1997, 530). RFRA, on the other hand, was not remedial legislation because there was no account of widespread religious discrimination by state and local governments, making such a far-reaching law unnecessary. As a result, Kennedy concluded, the legislation violated the principle of federalism because it was a "considerable congressional intrusion into the

States' traditional prerogatives and general authority to regulate for the health and welfare of their citizens" (*Boerne* 1997, 534).

There were three separate dissents to the majority opinion: Justice O'Connor, because *Boerne* was based on the premise that *Smith* was correct; Justice Breyer, who noted that reargument of *Smith* was necessary; and Justice Souter, who also called for a reargument and reconsideration of *Smith*. Notably, however, each member of the Court explicitly or implicitly endorsed Kennedy's limited view of Congress's enforcement power under the Fourteenth Amendment. However, neither the majority decision nor the dissents satisfactorily described when legislation was considered sufficiently "remedial" to withstand scrutiny by the Court, thus leaving Congress little guidance for the future.

Boerne is a significant restriction of Congress's power to respond to unfavorable Supreme Court decisions. In striking down RFRA the Court also eliminated the "substantive rights" theory implied in its 1966 *Morgan* decision, which had previously been invoked to validate congressional action to independently provide greater protection for civil rights and liberties under the Constitution when the Court was unwilling to do so. Also notable was the majority's pointed reminder to Congress of its supremacy in the realm of constitutional interpretation. The Court, obviously stinging from Congress's rebuke of *Smith*, appeared to jealously protect its self-anointed role as the ultimate expositor of the Constitution. In so doing the Court restricted Congress's role, as a coordinate branch of government, to independently participate in a discussion about the protection of civil rights and liberties in America. This conversation, according to the Court, must only take place on the Court's terms. In practical terms, the decision thus empowered only the Court, and not Congress, with the ability to protect religious liberty in America from potential infringements by state and local governments.

THE RELIGIOUS LIBERTY PROTECTION ACT

But *Boerne* would not be the last word in this ongoing conversation about religious freedom between Congress and the Court. Congress has responded to the Court's latest rebuke by reasserting its role in this constitutional conversation and continuing its exploration into a legislative remedy to *Smith*. Days after the *Boerne* decision, the House Subcommittee on Civil and Constitutional Rights announced that Congress would reopen the discussion about how Congress could address *Smith* and protect religious freedom. This led to several congressional hearings about how RFRA could be redrafted to withstand scrutiny by a Supreme Court quickly becoming known for its restrictions on congressional power and protection of states' rights.

After a year of discussion, led by the Coalition for the Free Exercise of Religion, constitutional law scholars, and members of Congress, over how Congress could enact legislation to protect religious exercise, the Religious Liberty

Protection Act was introduced in Congress. The measure was similar to RFRA in its reestablishment of the compelling government interest test to religious liberty cases involving neutral, generally applicable laws; but it relied on Congress's Article I spending power, which would apply to situations where the burden is the result of "a program or activity operated by the government that receives Federal financial assistance," and its power over commerce, which would reach activities where the burden "affects interstate commerce." A separate section of the bill also relied on section 5 of the Fourteenth Amendment in those instances where Congress could prove a pattern of religious discrimination, thus illustrating that the legislation was indeed "remedial." RLPA's authors were hopeful that the legislation was on firmer constitutional ground than RFRA, because if enacted, the Supreme Court would undoubtedly weigh in on its constitutionality.

However, there were some costs associated with the use of Congress's Article I power to justify RLPA. Some members of the Coalition for the Free Exercise of Religion and some members of Congress were opposed to the use of the commerce and spending clauses to protect religious freedom, and after a short time, support for RLPA began to diminish. Also, several groups, most notably civil rights organizations, began to lobby for exemptions to the measure, which they believed could be used to undermine civil rights legislation at the state and local levels. The Religious Liberty Protection Act died in Congress at the end of the session. The bill was reintroduced the following year, and in June of 1999, after an intensive lobbying effort on the part of the Coalition for the Free Exercise of Religion, the House passed RLPA by a voice vote. Attention moved to the Senate; however other news that week dampened the spirits of RLPA backers. On the last day of its term, the Supreme Court issued a trio of rulings that significantly cut back on congressional power. The decisions concerned challenges to federal legislation that allowed citizens to initiate private lawsuits against states in state courts. In each case, *Alden v. Maine* (1999), *Florida Prepaid Postsecondary Education Expense Board v. College Savings Bank* (1999), and *College Savings Bank v. Florida* (1999), the Court ruled against Congress and in favor of the states. The decisions extended a trend that began with the Court's 1992 ruling in *New York v. United States* (1992), where the Court curbed congressional power. In terms of the RLPA discussion, the decisions cast doubt on whether any congressional action to protect religious liberty would withstand the scrutiny of the Supreme Court. In the short term, the decisions stalled the forward momentum of the bill, and, despite the call of influential senators that passage of religious freedom legislation is a priority, the Senate has yet to take up RLPA in the 106th Congress (1999–2000). Moreover, the Supreme Court continues to show signs that it will continue this trend of cutting back congressional power in favor of states' rights. At the end of the term the Court is expected to strike down portions of the Americans with Disabilities Act and the Violence Against Women Act as a violation of states' sovereignty.

CONCLUSION

For the last decade, Congress has doggedly attempted to protect religious liberty at a time when the Supreme Court appears unwilling to do so. There is strong bipartisan support for a statutory solution to *Smith* to provide some level of protection against infringements by neutral and generally applicable federal, state, and local laws that burden an individual's religious exercise. Members of Congress have been vocal in their opposition of *Smith* and persistent in their efforts to find a solution, although at times there have been disagreements about what form this solution might take. From the beginning of this conversation Congress has asserted that the free exercise of religion is a right worthy of the highest level of protection, regardless of the Court's opinion on this matter.

In the process, Congress has engaged in a spirited conversation about the meaning of the free exercise guarantee of the First Amendment, and the right of Congress, as a coordinate branch of government, to assert its rightful role in deliberation of the meaning of the Constitution. Legislators did not set out to undermine the Court's role as one of many constitutional interpreters; rather they have been fighting to take their rightful place at the table to engage in this conversation. Overwhelming disapproval of *Smith* and widespread support for the Religious Freedom Restoration Act, the amendments to the American Indian Religious Freedom Act, and the Religious Liberty Protection Act provides evidence that many others share this perspective, and illustrates the need to open up this conversation beyond the Supreme Court. At the very least, there seems to be consensus in America about the need to protect religious liberty.

As a representative branch of government, Congress brings institutional strengths to this conversation about the Constitution that do not exist on the Supreme Court. Congress can take the pulse of the American public and reflect its will in its legislative proposals. Moreover, its manner of deliberating legislation provides the opportunity for groups such as the Coalition for the Free Exercise of Religion and the American Indian Religious Freedom Coalition to also participate in the legislative process.

Ultimately, encouraging and recognizing the role of multiple constitutional interpreters provides the country with multiple avenues for the protection of individual rights and liberties. It provides a country that values individual liberty with a second, or a third, or a fourth opportunity to thoroughly discuss this issue in an attempt to get it right. If one branch of government fails to adequately protect constitutional rights, then there is always the possibility that another branch will do so. Thus, having more participants involved in the process of constitutional interpretation ensures the greatest amount of protection for constitutional freedoms. The fact that constitutional interpretation is a constantly evolving process should provide reason enough for multiple constitutional interpreters. The fact that one of those liberties being protected is religious liberty, the "first freedom" for most Americans, provides another. As Louis Fisher concludes in chapter two of this volume, there is never a "final word" on the meaning of the Constitution, and the Court is not strong enough to impose its will on the other branches of government and the people, especially when there is overwhelming disagreement with the Court. This conversation about the Court, Congress, and religious liberty best illustrates how constitutional interpretation is a dynamic and constantly evolving process.

NOTES

1. See also *Black v. Employment Division*, 301 Or. 221 (1986). The use of peyote as a sacrament is a central tenant of the beliefs and practices of the Native American Church. For further information, see Omer Stewart, *Peyote Religion: A History* (Norman, Okla.: University of Oklahoma Press, 1987), and Edward F. Anderson, *Peyote, The Divine Cactus* (Tucson, Ariz.: University of Arizona Press, 1996).

2. ADAPT's alcohol and drug policy reads, "[m]isuse of alcohol and/or mind altering substances by a staff member is grounds for termination." In response to this case, ADAPT's executive director, John Gardin, stated, "We would have taken the same action had the claimant consumed wine at a Catholic ceremony or any drug anywhere. It would be the same result" *Smith* (1986), 209–211.

3. Oregon Revised Statutes provides that if an employee is terminated for misconduct, unemployment benefits are not available. Or. Rev. Stat. § 675.176(2)(a) (1987) states: "An individual shall be disqualified from the receipt of benefits if the authorized representative designated by the assistant director finds that the individual . . . has been discharged for misconduct connected with work." Or. Admin. R. 471-30-038(3) (1986) defines misconduct as "an act that amounts to willful disregard of an employer's interest, or recurring negligence which demonstrates wrongful intent."

4. The Court noted, "The legality of ingesting peyote does not affect our analysis of the state's interest. The state's interest in denying unemployment benefits to a claimant discharged for religiously motivated misconduct must be found in the unemployment compensation statutes, not the criminal statutes proscribing the use of peyote" (*Smith* [1986], 219).

5. Justice Scalia explained that precedent cases outside the unemployment context where the Court applied the compelling government interest involved "hybrid" rights, which warranted use of a high level of scrutiny. "Earlier decisions authorizing exemptions to neutral, generally applicable laws never concerned the free exercise clause alone, but rather, the free exercise clause in combination with other constitutional guarantees." He also differentiated *Smith* from the precedent unemployment compensation cases because they did not involve "an across-the-board criminal prohibition on a particular form of conduct" (*Smith* [1990] 881–2).

6. The Court ruled that two free exercise cases involving religious liberty challenges to prison regulations and military regulations were of such "special circumstances" that the Court should defer to the judgment of military and prison personnel (*Goldman v. Weinberger* and *O'Lone v. Estate of Shabazz* 482 U.S. 342 [1987]). It, therefore, used "rationality review" rather than the compelling government interest test to evaluate the religious liberty challenge.

7. The Court concluded that the regulation that prohibited the wearing of headgear indoors, which was challenged by an Orthodox Jew who was reprimanded for wearing a yarmulke, was "reasonable" and was administered in an even-handed fashion, and thus did not violated the free exercise of the Constitution. In response, Congress enacted Public Law 100-180, which allows the wearing of neat and conservative religious headgear indoors if it does not interfere with a person's military duties.

8. This has been referred to as the "one-way ratchet theory." Congress can act to expand rights beyond the Court's definition, but cannot dilute those rights. This theory has been upheld as late as 1982 by the Court in *Mississippi University for Women v. Hogan*, 458 U.S. 718 (1982).

9. On April 29, 1994, President Clinton addressed Indian leaders at the White House and signed a governmental directive to all heads of executive departments and agencies to work cooperatively with tribal governments to have access to sacred eagles and parts.

CHAPTER SEVEN

The Least Dangerous Branch? The Supreme Court's New Judicial Activism

JOHN F. STACK JR. AND COLTON C. CAMPBELL

Whoever attentively considers the different departments of power must perceive that in a government in which they are separated from each other, the judiciary, from the nature of its functions, will always be the least dangerous to the political rights of the constitution; because it will be least in a capacity to annoy or injure them.

—Alexander Hamilton, *Federalist Paper* No. 78

Viewed from the perspective of the new century, federal–state relations are emerging in new and, perhaps, unexpected ways. Central to the revitalized power of states is the Supreme Court's new activism. Such judicial activism is not new; it is inherent in the nature of judicial decision making. Chief Justice John Marshall, with scant authority (reliance on Blackstone's treatise on the Law of England), with a deliberate omission of the second sentence within article III, section 2, paragraph 2 of the U.S. Constitution ("With such exceptions and such regulations as the Congress shall make"), and with exhortation to construe a positive grant of power as negative of any additional powers (the *negative implications doctrine*), invalidated section E of the Judiciary Act of 1789, establishing the Court's right to overturn an act of Congress deemed inconsistent with the Constitution. *Marbury v. Madison* (1803), therefore, declares that it is emphatically the province of the judicial department to say what the law is under a Constitution that is acknowledged in Article VI to be the supreme law of the land.

The reach of *Marbury v. Madison* resonates through American politics. It establishes the rule of law as the basis of legitimacy in the American political system. No person, no group, no institution can stand above it (*Cooper v. Aaron*

[1958]; *United States v. Nixon* [1974]; *Clinton v. Jones* [1997]). Alternatively, this landmark case illustrates the double-edged sword of judicial activism—the court as an instrument of political, social, or ideological change within the context of American political institutions. When in 1857, the Supreme Court nullified the anti-slavery portion of the Missouri Compromise in *Dred Scott v. Sandford* (1857), the Civil War became virtually inevitable. Activism does not guarantee wise, prudent, or socially efficacious judgments, but it is increasingly a hallmark of Supreme Court decision making in the twentieth century. This means that an elitist, non-elected branch of government, insulated from direct popular pressure (e.g., federal judges who are granted life-tenure based on good behavior and whose salaries cannot be reduced, Article III, section 1), stands in contrast to the popularly elected legislative branch. Federal judges are by no means immune from congressional or executive pressures often far short of the drastic constitutionally mandated removal procedure known as impeachment.

Alexander Hamilton's oft-quoted counsel that the judiciary is the "least dangerous branch" (*Federalist* No. 78) perhaps inadvertently suggests that politics and judicial decision making are strange bedfellows. We suggest quite the opposite. Judicial activism is often a manifestation of the judiciary's disquietude with the status quo.

In a series of recent cases the Rehnquist Court has recharged state sovereignty in unexpected and surprisingly energetic ways. Here, we analyze the flip side of congressional–judicial relations: the reinvigorated agenda of the least dangerous branch in reducing what may seem to be unchallengeable federal prerogatives. It is worth noting that the judiciary is an inherently political body that does not exist in a vacuum; the Rehnquist Court has moved to constrain congressional prerogatives in a number of important ways (O'Brien 2000e).

RESTORING THE TENTH AMENDMENT

Ratified in 1791 as part of the Bill of Rights, the Tenth Amendment specifies that "the powers not delegated to the United States by the Constitution, nor prohibited by it to the States, are reserved to the States respectively, or to the people." Of all the amendments demanded by the anti-Federalists in the state conventions that ratified the Constitution, one calling for a reserved powers clause was the most common. However, initial erosion of the Tenth Amendment began early in the twentieth century. In 1895 Congress passed an act forbidding the shipment of lottery tickets in interstate commerce. The purpose was only nominally a regulation of commerce: its real purpose was to restrict gambling, a matter that had always been the exclusive domain of the states. In *Champion v. Ames* (1903), by a fractious five-to-four decision, the Supreme Court upheld the act.

The following year the Court, in *McCray v. United States* (1904), upheld a congressional act imposing a prohibitive excise tax on oleomargarine. This action amounted to an exercise of a police power to protect the health of the citizenry, under the guise of a constitutional exercise of the power to levy taxes for "general welfare," as provided in Article I, section 8 (McDonald 1992).

The increasing assertiveness of Congress and state legislatures in addressing complex issues of labor/management relations, and in attempting to protect workers from the excesses of industrial life, caused the Supreme Court to revitalize the Tenth Amendment. The Court used the Tenth Amendment in conjunction with the Fourteenth Amendment's due-process clause as a way of limiting the activism of states and Congress. It also underscored the Court's solicitude for state sovereignty as a way to escape the encroachment of activist state and federal legislatures. In *Lochner v. New York* (1905) the New York legislature passed a law limiting the hours and other working conditions for bakers. In his dissent, made famous by time and changing views of judicial activism, and Congress's increasing reliance on cooperative federalism, Justice Oliver Wendell Holmes denounced the activism of the Court:

> This case is decided upon an economic theory which a large part of the country does not entertain. . . . The Fourteenth Amendment does not enact Mr. Herbert Spencer's Social Statics. . . . It is settled by various decisions of this court that state constitutions and state laws may regulate life in many ways which we as legislators might think as injudicious or if you like as tyrannical as this, and which equally with this interfere with the liberty to contract. Sunday laws and usury laws are ancient examples. A more modern one is the prohibition of lotteries. . . . But a constitution is not intended to embody a particular economic theory, whether of paternalism and the organic relation of the citizen to the State or of *laissez faire.* It is made for people of fundamentally differing views, and the accident of our finding certain opinions natural and familiar or novel and even shocking ought not to conclude our judgment upon the question whether statutes embodying them conflict with the Constitution of the United States. (*Lochner v. New York* 1905, 546)

The Lochner Court's application of substantive due process, however, provided states and the federal government with some degree of latitude in safeguarding traditional concerns in the area of police powers, such as the health, safety, morals, and welfare of citizens (see *Jacobson v. Massachusetts* [1905] upholding a state law requiring smallpox vaccinations; *Muller v. Oregon* [1908] unanimously upholding a ten-hour-a-day state law for women working in industries; O'Brien 2000a, 943–44). But the Court's interpretation of the Fourteenth Amendment's due-process clause, and its insistence on dual federalism, runs strong in a series of major decisions (for example, see: *Adair v. United States* [1908] overturning a federal labor relations statute banning yellow-dog contracts; *Coppage v. Kansas* [1915] invalidating state law prohibiting yellow-dog contracts; *Adkins v. Children's Hospital* [1923] overturning the District of Columbia's minimum-wage law for women; O'Brien 2000a, 944–46).

This activist posture by the Court led to confrontation with the executive branch during 1937 when the Court overturned virtually all of the major programs of the New Deal (see *A.L.A. Schechter Poultry Corp. v. United States* [1935] striking down the National Industrial Recovery Act; *United States v. Butler* [1936] striking down the Agriculture Adjustment Act). Overall, nearly 200 laws (both state and federal) were struck down between 1897 and 1937 (O'Brien 2000a, 258). (See photo 7.1.)

With Franklin D. Roosevelt's threat to pack the Court, increasing the number of seats to fifteen in 1937, the Court's conservative bare-majority (five-member coalition) collapsed, signaling a dramatic reassessment of the role of Congress in *West Coast Hotel v. Parrish* (1937), endorsing state wage and hour restrictions and expressly overturning *Adkins v. Children's Hospital.* In the ensuing fifty-five years (1937 to 1992), the Supreme Court overturned only one statute that violated the Tenth Amendment and that decision, itself, was later overturned.

THE TENTH AMENDMENT: A SECOND CUT

Under the Tenth Amendment the Rehnquist Court has moved toward a dual federalist approach long abandoned since the late 1930s. For the most conservative members of the Supreme Court, the Tenth Amendment increasingly became a means of reviving state interests amid the harsh realities of the modern administrative state. The complexity of modern government, the requirements of extensive regulatory laws, an integrated economy, and the necessity of federal oversight seemingly made federal-dominated cooperative federalism, with its emphasis on centralized control, inevitable. However, the conservatism introduced into national politics by the Reagan administration is reflected in a Supreme Court that increasingly adheres to conservative principles. While judicial activism has traditionally fallen outside the sanctioned parameters of conservative orthodoxy, a bare majority of the Rehnquist Court (Chief Justice Rehnquist and Associate Justices O'Connor, Scalia, Kennedy, and Thomas) is pioneering new interpretations, theories, and tests that challenge established principles of federalism. These challenges include circumscribing federal authority in areas of interstate commerce and the sovereign immunity of states. (See photo 7.2.)

At present, an embracing conservatism has not yet fully emerged for members of the Rehnquist majority, as many commentators and analysts of the Court

Photo 7.1   The members of the Supreme Court between March 14, 1932 and June 2, 1937. Photo taken by Harris and Ewing, collection of the Supreme Court of the United States

Photo 7.2   The Rehnquist Court, 1994–present. Photo taken by Richard Strauss, Smithsonian Institution, collection of the Supreme Court of the United States

predicted. Judges, even Supreme Court justices, are constrained by the facts and issues presented in each case before them. Deference to previously decided cases—the doctrine of stare decisis—remains a basic part of how the Supreme Court functions. But beginning in 1976 in *National League of Cities v. Usery* (1976), the Court's new conservative justices have increasingly tried to restore the Tenth Amendment as a substantive limitation on Congress's commerce powers (Scheiber 1992). There is by no means one principal philosophical trajectory, but in the last two decades, a body of law and political philosophy has coalesced around the ideas attributed to, or associated with, the Tenth Amendment.

For many students of the Court, *National League of Cities v. Usery* was a surprising bellwether of a policy change in Commerce Clause jurisprudence (Foster and Leeson 1998). Moribund since the Court's rejection of dual federalism in the late 1930s, a six-to-three majority brought back to life an affirmative limitation on Congress's power to regulate economic relationships, articulating a new approach to federal–state relations. The Court voided a 1974 amendment to the Fair Labor Standards Act (FSLA), an act to expand federal minimum-wage provisions and maximum hours to state and local government employees. Rehnquist, an associate justice at the time, explained that those provisions made more expensive state and local governments' basic and traditional functions—for example, police protection (O'Brien 2000a, 681). While acknowledging that the Tenth Amendment had been initially defined as a "truism," Rehnquist noted that Congress could not "exercise power in a fashion that impaired the States' integrity or their ability to function effectively in a federal system" (*National League of Cities v. Usery, 842 citing Fry, Fry v. United States* [1975]). In stating a revitalized approach to dual federalism, Rehnquist reaffirmed the sovereignty that inheres in the nature of states:

> We have repeatedly recognized that there are attributes of sovereignty attaching to every state government which may not be impaired by Congress not because Congress may lack an affirmative grant of legislative authority to reach the matter, but because the Constitution prohibits it from exercising the authority in that manner. (*National League of Cities v. Usery* 1976, 845)

Rehnquist pointed to a state's ability to locate the seat of government or to determine how the seat of government may be changed as an example of the "separate and independent existence" of state sovereignty (*National League of Cities v. Usery* 1976, 845–46). Such functions, he interpreted, fell within the "plenary authority" of states (*National League of Cities v. Usery* 1976, 845–46). This decision elevated "a state's sovereignty to the level of constitutional law," thus limiting the intrusive power of Congress under the Interstate Commerce Clause (O'Brien 2000a, 683).

In his concurrence Justice Blackmun endorsed the Court's balancing approach as it addressed "the relationship between the Federal Government and our States" (*National League of Cities v. Usery* 1976, 856). The decision, he noted, did not "outlaw federal power" in an area like environmental protection where federal interests necessarily predominate over those of the states (*National League of Cities v. Usery* 1976, 856).

In his dissent Justice Brennan characterized the decision as a "patent usurpation of the role reserved for the political process by their purported discovery in the Constitution of a restraint derived from sovereignty of the States on Congress's exercise of the commerce power" (*National League of Cities v. Usery* 1976, 542). Seeing the 1974 amendments as "an entirely legitimate exercise of the commerce power," and not prohibited by any theory of "state sovereignty" recognized by the Court, Brennan strenuously opposed the Court's decision (*National League of Cities v. Usery* 1976, 871). Further, Brennan stated that the Court "manufactured an abstraction without substance founded neither in the words of the Constitution nor on precedent," a concept made "no less pernicious" by characterizing the 1974 amendments "as legislation directed against the 'States qua States'" (*National League of Cities v. Usery* 1976, 858).

National League of Cities v. Usery proved difficult to apply, however, because it opened up so many problems in its application (McDonald 1992). One such problem was that the distinction between "traditional" and "essential" state activities, central to the Court's attempt to reinvigorate state sovereignty, were never adequately defined (O'Brien 2000a, 683). This case did not provide a justification as to why the Court, rather than Congress, should defend state sovereignty (O'Brien 200a, 683). The coalition supporting *Usery* disintegrated when Justice Blackmun reversed himself in *Garcia v. San Antonio Metropolitan Transportation Authority* (1985) and overruled *National League of Cities v. Usery*.

In her dissenting opinion, Justice O'Connor expressed concern about increasing congressional power to regulate interstate commerce, gradually erasing the diffusion of power between the federal government and the states (*Garcia v. San Antonio* 1985, 584). States' inability to perform constitutionally mandated functions, she said, was rooted in the seemingly relentless power that industrialization, combined with transportation and communication systems as well as "unprecedented growth of federal regulatory activity," confers on interstate commerce. Citing federal mandates dictating the retirement age of state law-enforcement personnel, and an increasing maze of regulatory laws, O'Connor indicated the failure of the political process to protect states against federal encroachment. "With the abandonment of *National League of Cities*," she declared, "all that stands between the remaining essentials of state sovereignty and Congress is the latter's undeveloped capacity for self-restraint" (*Garcia v. San Antonio* 1985, 588).

THE TENTH AMENDMENT RISING

The Supreme Court's review of the Gun-Free School Zones Act of 1990 is another example of the Court's more exacting standard of judicial review of congressional actions, even under Article I's powerful interstate commerce authority. Responding to studies showing that, in 1987, more than half a million students carried guns to school, lawmakers sought to turn the tide against firearm violence and drug activity. Part of the act prohibited an individual from possessing a firearm at a place that the individual knew, or had reasonable cause to believe, was a school zone: grounds of any public, private, or parochial school, or property within one thousand feet of such premises. Violators were subject to penalties up to five years in prison and a $5,000 fine.

During congressional hearings on the Gun-Free School Zones Act, many witnesses testified about the impact of increasing violence involving firearms on the nation's educational system. However, none specifically discussed the effects on interstate commerce. Neither the statute nor its legislative history contained express findings about the constitutional source of Congress's authority to enact the legislation (Foster and Leeson 1998).

United States v. Lopez (1995) signaled the first time since the New Deal that the Court found Congress to have exceeded its constitutional discretion to regulate interstate commerce—in this case, the movement of guns across state lines that could end up in school playgrounds (Greenhouse 1999). Alfonso Lopez, Jr., a twelfth-grade student at Edison High School in San Antonio, Texas, took a concealed .38 caliber handgun loaded with five bullets to school. Upon confrontation with school authorities, Lopez admitted to carrying a weapon, explaining that the gun was given to him by another student for use after school in a "gang war." Lopez also told officials that he was to receive forty dollars for delivering the gun. Lopez was arrested and charged under Texas law with firearm possession on school grounds. The following day, the state charges were dismissed after federal agents charged the teenager with violating the 1990 Gun-Free School Zones Act.

Central to the holding in *Lopez* was Chief Justice Rehnquist's reliance on a revitalized concept of dual federalism. The Constitution, he argued, creates a federal government of enumerated powers; citing James Madison, "the powers delegated by the proposed Constitution to the federal government are few and defined, period. Those which are to remain in the State governments are numerous and indefinite" (*United States v. Lopez* [1995], 552). Rehnquist then underscored the constitutionally mandated division of authority within the nature of federalism designed "to ensure protection of our fundamental liberties" (citing *Gregory v. Ashcroft* [1991]). He elevated dual federalism to the status afforded the separation and independence of these coordinate branches of the federal government, stating: "to prevent the accumulation of excessive power in any one branch, a healthy balance of power between the States and the Federal Government will reduce the risk of tyranny and abuse from either front" (*United States v. Lopez* 1995, 552, citing *Gregory v. Ashcroft*, 458).

In a series of five-to-four decisions, members of the Rehnquist Court again invoked the Tenth Amendment to limit congressional power in *Printz v. United States* and *Mack v. United States* (1997). These cases emanated from Congress's adoption of the Brady Handgun Violence Prevention Act of 1993, which amended the 1968 Gun Control Act by requiring the attorney general to establish a national instant criminal background check system by November 30, 1998. "It is incontestable that the Constitution established a system of 'dual sovereignty,' " Justice Scalia stated for the majority in sharply rebuking Congress's attempt to define the limits of state authority (*Printz v. United States* and *Mack v. United States* 1997, citing *Gregory v. Ashcroft* [1991]).

Scalia articulated a compelling vision of dual federalism, asserting that the Constitution "contemplates that a State's government will represent and remain accountable to its own citizens" (*Printz v. United States* 1997, 2377, citing *New York v. United States* 1992). This design, which he called a "great innovation," afforded American citizens a political system based on "two orders of government," possessing "its own direct relationship, its privity, its own set of mutual rights and obligations to the people who sustain it and are governed by it" (*Printz v. United States* 1997, 2377, citing *U.S. Term Limits, Inc. v. Thornton* [1995], Justice Kennedy concurring). And once again, a conservative justice invoked the words of Madison: "The local or municipal authorities form distinct and independent portions of the supremacy, no more subject, within their respective spheres, to the general authority than the general authority is subject to them, within its own spheres" (*Printz v. United States* 1997, 2377).

THE TENTH AMENDMENT: A THIRD CUT

Perhaps the most telling dimensions of a revitalized concept of state sovereignty and a concomitant limitation on Congress's lawmaking authority are demonstrated in two very recent cases. In these cases the Supreme Court dramatically expands the concept of the sovereign immunity of states by drawing on the Tenth Amendment and gives new life to the Eleventh Amendment. The Eleventh Amendment, which became part of the Constitution on January 8, 1798, by a presidential message to Congress, restricts the power of federal courts to hear suits against states brought by citizens of other states or by aliens. It is one of only two amendments that expressly repudiate a Supreme Court decision, in this case, *Chisholm v. Georgia* (1793).

In *Alden v. Maine* (1999), the Court, in yet another divided five-to-four decision, immunized a state from litigation filed in the courts of that state pursuing the enforcement of federal relief against the state. Probation officers in the state of Maine attempted to secure a federal right to be compensated for working overtime. Justice Kennedy, writing for the Court, boldly held that "the powers delegated to Congress under Article I of the United States Constitution do not include the power to subject nonconsenting States to private suits for damages in state courts" (*Alden v. Maine* 1999, 653). In dismissing the claim of Maine's probation officers the Court reasoned that since Maine "had not consented to suits for overtime pay and liquidated damages" under the Fair Labor Standards Act, Congress lacked the power under Article I "to subject nonconsenting states to private suits for damages in state courts" (*Alden v. Maine* 1999, 2246). The Court broke new ground in defining additional limits on congressional and constitutional intrusion into the sovereign affairs of states.

Central to the Supreme Court's holding was the assertion that the Constitution defends state sovereignty in two ways. First, the "Nation's primary sovereignty" flows to states accompanied by the "dignity and essential attributes inhering" in that sovereign state. States "form distinct and independent portions of the supremacy, no more subject, within their respective spheres, to the general authority than the general authority is subject to them within its own sphere," declared Justice Kennedy while quoting *Federalist* No. 39 (*Alden v. Maine* 1999, 2247). Second, the Court's assessment went even further regarding the nature of dual federalism, stating that even as to concerns about the "competence of the National Government," the national constitutional framework "secures the founding generation's rejection of 'the concept of a central government that would act upon and through States' in favor of 'a system in which the State and Federal Governments would exercise concurrent authority over the people—who were, in Hamilton's words, 'the only proper objects of government'" (*Alden v. Maine* 1999, 2247, citing *Printz v. United States* 1997, 919–920). The residuary and inviolable sovereignty of the state, therefore, remains and is "not redelegated to the role of mere provinces or political corporations, but retain(s) the dignity, though not the full authority, of sovereignty" (*Alden v. Maine* 1999, 2247).

Federal power was also at issue in *Kimel v. Florida Board of Regents* (2000). The Age Discrimination in Employment Act of 1967 (ADEA) subjected states to suits by individuals by outlawing employer discrimination against any individual with respect to his or her compensation. The ambit of ADEA's coverage was expanded over the years by amendment, ultimately embracing the treatment of state employers and employees. A number of current and former faculty members and librarians at Florida State University and Florida International University sued the Florida Board of Regents (BOR) when the BOR refused to require the two state universities to allocate funds to provide previously agreed-upon market adjustments to the salaries of eligible university employees. The unwillingness of the universities to provide funds, it was contended, offended the ADA and the Florida Civil Rights Act of 1992 (*Kimel v. Florida Board of Regents* 2000, 534).

The Court's analysis proceeded on two fronts. In the first instance, the Court applied a "simple but stringent test." "Congress," Justice O'Connor argued, "may abrogate the State's constitutionally secured immunity from suit and federal court only by making its intentions unmistakably clear in the language of the statute" (*Kimel v. Florida Board of Regents* 2000, 640, citing *Dellmuth v. Muth* [1989]; drawing on the Court's earlier decision in *Seminole Tribe of Florida v. Florida* [1996]). The Court declared that Congress under Article I does not possess the power to "abrogate" a state's sovereign immunity. "Even when the Constitution vests in Congress complete lawmaking authority over a particular area," declared O'Connor, "the Eleventh Amendment prevents congressional authorization of suits by private parties against unconsenting States" (*Seminole Tribe of Florida v. Florida* 1996, 72). In a clear attempt to compel congressional acquiescence in *Seminole Tribe v. Florida*, the majority stated that Congress could not "extract constructive waivers of sovereign immunity" via Article I powers. Thus, the Court sought to close what it considered to be a loophole implicit in Article I's commerce power (*Kimel v. Florida Board of Regents* 2000, 643).

The Court's logic also extended to consideration of section 5 of the Fourteenth Amendment, which states: "the Congress shall have power to enforce, by appropriate legislation, the provisions of this article." This gave Congress the authority to abrogate a state's sovereign immunity. Here the Court relied on its recent decision in *City of Boerne v. Flores* (1997) interpreting section 5 as an affirmative grant of power to Congress. "It is for Congress in the first instance to 'determine whether and what legislation is needed to secure the guarantees of the Fourteenth Amendment,' and its conclusions are entitled to much deference," stated Justice O'Connor (*City of Boerne v. Flores* 1997, 536).

Invoking the *negative implications doctrine*, the Court reasoned that the enforcement provision of section 5 of the Fourteenth Amendment also "serves to limit that power" (*City of Boerne v. Flores* 1997, 644). Justice O'Connor went on to declare: "The ultimate interpretation and determination of the Fourteenth Amendment's substantive meaning remains the province of the judicial branch." Drawing on the "congruence and proportionality tests" of *City of Boerne* (*Kimel v. Florida Board of Regents* 2000, 645–47), the Court declared that state-based age discrimination did not violate the Fourteenth Amendment if "the age classification in question is rationally related to a legitimate state interest. The rationality commanded by the Equal Protection Clause does not require states to match age distinctions and legitimate interests they serve with razorlike precision" (*Kimel v. Florida Board of Regents* 2000, 543).

CONCLUSION

The Rehnquist Court has pushed far beyond its initial concern with the nature of federal–state relations as expressed in *National League of Cities v. Usery* (1976). Utilizing the revived Tenth Amendment, and repeatedly drawing on relatively new and novel readings of original intent, the Court has pioneered a new interpretation, indeed, one might say, a new constitutional approach to federalism—one that clearly conceptualizes new understandings of the nature of the sovereignty of states within American constitutional history and politics.

We suggest that the Court's willingness to move beyond the Tenth Amendment, and to fuse it with the Eleventh Amendment, is significant because of the expanding protection afforded state prerogatives under revitalized theories of dual federalism. The Eleventh Amendment cases are, therefore, striking because they erect a further barrier to federal intrusion in the sovereign affairs of states.

Chief Justice John Marshall declared in *McCulloch v. Maryland* (1819), that the power to tax constitutes the power to destroy. The power to initiate litigation against a state is, perhaps, a late twentieth-century, early twenty-first-century power of equivalent magnitude. The willingness to combine Tenth and Eleventh Amendment concerns may represent a shrewd attempt to construct a constitutional platform that will radiate outward. The study of constitutional law in the twentieth century is also preeminently the story of increasing federal authority under Article I powers, most notably the interstate commerce clause in both civil and criminal law, as well as the nearly transcendent powers of the Fourteenth Amendment. That the Court has sought to constrict section 5 of the Fourteenth Amendment may constitute as significant a breakthrough as the Warren Court's selective incorporation of the Bill of Rights. As *City of Boerne v. Flores* (1997) and *Kimel v. Florida Board of Regents* (2000) illustrate, the next major constitutional horizon may be found in the progressive narrowing of substantive rights guaranteed by the Fourteenth Amendment. In this respect, the Court's activist interpretation of section 5 of the Fourteenth Amendment is something far more important than the mere procedural adjustment to issues of substantial constitutional weight.

We argue that the Rehnquist Court's activism is not new in the context of American constitutional law; the twentieth century witnessed several periods of judicial activism. Notable, however, is the Rehnquist Court's approach to issues of constitutional interpretation. It is often systematic, coherent, and detailed in its assessment of history, philosophy, and procedural attempts to turn back the expansive power of Congress. The opinions considered above resonate as well a sense of passion. These principles are rooted in a political conservatism and a judicial activism that gives expression to fundamental concerns about the erosion of political participation as epitomized in state sovereignty that much of contemporary economics, technology, law, and philosophy tend to overwhelm.

PART THREE

Toward Institutional Comity

CHAPTER EIGHT

When Do Courts "Legislate"? Reflections on Congress and the Court

NICOL C. RAE

"The Supreme Court follows the election returns," "the least dangerous branch," "the imperial judiciary"—these are just some of the more common phrases that scholars have used to encapsulate the relationship between the legislative and judicial branches in American government. That these maxims contradict each other might be taken to indicate a profound scholarly confusion over the degree to which the Court participates in the legislative process. Yet the contradictions are due less to confusion than to the fact that the role of the Court in lawmaking has oscillated dramatically from one era of America history to another. Carolyn Long's depiction of the disputes between Congress and the Supreme Court on religious freedom issues in recent decades as "a conversation" among "multiple constitutional interpreters" could be extended to the relationship between the branches per se.

The first three articles of the Constitution and the buttressing of the Supreme Court's role by the *Marbury v. Madison* (1803) decision has left the legislative process a perpetually contested terrain in American government, giving the judiciary a degree of legislative authority that is almost unique in the annals of democratic government. But while the essays in this volume demonstrate that in certain circumstances the lawmaking authority has passed to the federal courts under the power of "judicial review," they also indicate that this is an intermittent but not a permanent phenomenon. These reflections will attempt to delineate the circumstances in which the Court has played a significant legislative role and will likely do so again in the twenty-first century. As we shall see, these situations have little to do with the merits of particular issues or pieces of legislation in question, but much more to do with the extent to which either the legislative or judicial branch reflects the consensus of American public opinion at a particular point in time.

The first issue that we need to dispose of, however, is the rather tiresome and unfruitful debate over "judicial activism" and its converse "judicial restraint." As far as judicial activism is concerned it appears that nobody approves of it in the abstract (except perhaps for several law professors and the occasional candidly aristocratic justices) but everybody does it when the opportunity presents itself. It is certainly "activist" for the Court to lead the country in a new direction as, for example, the Warren Court did on a variety of issues. For a subsequent court to reverse that jurisprudence in the name of "judicial restraint" can, of course, also be depicted as "activist" by those who disapprove of the policy change, as has happened with some of the "federalism" decisions of the Rehnquist Court discussed in the chapters by O'Brien, and Stack and Campbell. Perhaps it is more useful to think in terms not of activism–restraint, but in terms of constraints or limits on the legislative activity of the Supreme Court. Within those limits it is clear that the Court has a great deal of scope not only to overrule the laws passed by the legislative branch, but to force Congress to address pertinent matters that it had hitherto been ignoring. On the other hand, once these limitations are breached, the countervailing forces in the American constitutional system move rapidly to put the Court in its place, as in President Franklin D. Roosevelt's confrontation with the Supreme Court in 1937 as well as in reaction to the Court's very liberal judgments in the late 1960s and early 1970s. The highly tentative, legalistic, and incremental nature of the Rehnquist Court's controversial federalism decisions is further testimony to the Court's awareness of these limitations.

Thus, while *Marbury v. Madison* still represents the ultimate example of political and constitutional legerdemain, *Dred Scott v. Sandford* (1857) stands as the quintessential example of judicial intervention, merely further inflaming a vexed political climate. Louis Fisher's chapter is a salutary reminder for a scholarly generation raised on debates over the "imperial judiciary" that the power of the Court is in fact limited by the powers of the other two branches of the federal government and, without the acquiescence of Long's other "constitutional interpreters," the Court will remain "the least dangerous" branch. Both Congress and the presidency can exercise considerable influence over the Court—the appointment and confirmation process, Congress's control over the structure of the federal judiciary and its jurisdiction in Article III, the reliance on the executive branch to enforce decisions—and, as Fisher shows us, they have not hesitated to use these powers to restrain the court at various points in U.S. history. Mary Volcansek's chapter also illustrates how another constitutional check on judicial "excesses"—the congressional impeachment power—has been used by legislators to make an example of "unreliable judges" and thereby influence judicial behavior.

Given these constraints on judicial power in what circumstances are we likely to see the Court effectively "legislate" by actively exercising its powers of judicial review, striking down the legislative acts of the other two branches? Looking at the course of American history, we can discern four scenarios in which we are likely to witness sustained legislative activism from the judicial branch. In the first two instances the Court is likely to succeed in setting a new direction in national public policy, but in the latter two the Court is likely to overstep the constraints on its political power and find itself checked by a backlash in public opinion expressed through the other two branches of government.

The first situation where the Supreme Court is likely to have leeway to change public policy occurs when the acts of Congress or state legislatures have gotten ahead of what popular public opinion is likely to bear. In fact, in these instances, the legislative branch, rather than the judiciary, may be acting before the time is ripe for change in public policy, and the Court reflects the broader consensus, checks the "excesses" of the legislative branch, with little cost to its own power. The clearest instance of this would be the 1890-to-1910 period when the Court succeeded in striking down progressive legislation such as the 1894 federal income tax (*Pollock v. Farmers' Loan & Trust Co.* 1895) and New York's wages and hours legislation (*Lochner v. New York* 1905), because the Court's views were more in tune with the laissez faire economic consensus of the time.

The second scenario for judicial policymaking occurs when Congress is either deadlocked or reluctant to act on a pressing issue of national concern, and only the Supreme Court can break the logjam and set a new course of policy in a particular area. Because national public opinion is ahead of Congress in this situation, the court-mandated change of direction is eventually likely to establish a new popular consensus on the issue, which will then later be reflected by congressional enactments. The classic example of this situation is, of course, the issue of civil rights in the 1950s. With Congress gridlocked by the power of the white South, the Court dramatically set the nation on the path to desegregation and the full enfranchisement of African Americans in its monumental 1954 *Brown v. Board of Education* decision. That decision not only emboldened the civil rights movement but also was eventually reflected in legislation by the Civil Rights Act of 1964 and the Voting Rights Act of 1965.

In the third set of circumstances, legislative activism by the Court is more likely to produce a massive political backlash and a serious threat to its institutional authority. This is when the Court is caught in a "time warp" with its membership reflecting a bygone national consensus during a period of deep change in national public policy. Of course the classic example of this situation is the New Deal era, when a Supreme Court composed of appointees from the laissez faire era proceeded to strike down major components of President Roosevelt's New Deal, principally the National Industrial Recovery Act, in its 1935 *Schechter*

Poultry Corp. v. United States decision. Following a landslide reelection together with the most overwhelmingly Democratic Congress of the century, Roosevelt (who had hitherto not had a single appointment to the Court) came up with a dramatic plan to alter the composition and the ideological majority of the Court. Roosevelt proposed legislation that would allow a president to nominate a new justice for every sitting justice over the age of seventy. His plan subsequently died in Congress but only after the Court dramatically switched its judgments to a more pro–New Deal stance. Then, as the sitting justices either died or retired, Roosevelt was eventually able to nominate an entire court by the time of his own death in 1945 and the judicial branch had given its imprimatur to the New Deal revolution. Nevertheless, the so-called Court-packing plan posed the most serious threat to the power and authority of the judicial branch since *Marbury v. Madison*, and exposed the potentially weak political position of the Court if it acted in defiance of the other two branches when the executive and the legislative reflected a public consensus for policy change.

The final situation in which the judiciary usurps the legislative power may be equally dangerous to the legitimacy of the Court. This is when an ideological majority (on some issues a very narrow majority) on the Court is not behind public opinion but too far ahead of it, and proceeds to overturn long-standing laws in the name of a "living constitution" or the Court's higher constitutional authority to protect rights and minorities. When this happens, unfortunately for the Court, it is likely to provoke a widespread popular backlash that will be reflected in the other branches of the federal government that are more responsive to the popular will, even if elite opinion is on the side of the Court. The decisions of the later Warren and early Burger courts clearly appear to fit this pattern, when the Supreme Court emboldened by its success in changing national policy on civil rights attempted to change state and federal law on matters such as criminal suspects' rights, school prayer, the death penalty, school busing, and abortion, when a national consensus for change was not yet apparent or on some of these issues (such as the death penalty and suspects' rights) was actually moving in the opposite direction. And while the Court may succeed in changing the law in defiance of a majority of the public, the sustained hostility engendered toward the legislative branch is not healthy for the Court's authority. A Supreme Court perceived as arrogant, elitist, and out-of-touch is unlikely to be respected. As a result of Court decisions in the 1968 election, America witnessed the unprecedented spectacle of two presidential candidates—Republican Richard Nixon and third-party protest candidate George Wallace—running against the Supreme Court, and between them winning almost 60 percent of the national popular vote. Indeed, it appeared that the Court's decisions played a key role in forging the Republican presidential majority of 1968 to 1992, and making the Court itself a perennial issue in presidential elections during that period.

The chapters by O'Brien, and Stack and Campbell argue that a similar situation may be arising with regard to the recent Tenth and Eleventh Amendment decisions of a slender five-to-four majority on the Rehnquist Court. To date, however, it is not fully apparent if the scenario of three decades ago is being repeated as the Rehnquist Court's majority to redefine federalism by interpreting the Constitution in a manner likely to give far more powers to the state governments, is narrow and tentative. If this constitutes another legislative revolution led from the judicial branch then it is a revolution by stealth, for the legalistic and incremental nature of the decisions themselves, and the generally low public profile to date of Tenth and Eleventh Amendment issues has entailed little danger of a significant public backlash against the Court. The Rehnquist-led majority has also been fortunate to face a Republican Congress since 1994 that has been largely in accord with what the Court has been doing. Defying a strong Democratic majority on Capitol Hill would be much more risky political endeavor for the Supreme Court.

So there clearly are circumstances in which the Court can effectively legislate, although unless it reads the public mood carefully, it is likely to find itself contesting for political authority on these matters with the other branches of government: a conflict that poses significant risks for the Court's authority. One further development of the past half-century or so demands our attention, however, because it has implications for the long-term authority of the Court and the integrity of the American political system as a whole. This development brings us back to the second of the scenarios above: the tendency for Congress to "pass the buck" to the Court on a whole range of political issues that the legislative branch itself is reluctant to tackle or resolve. Since *Brown v. Board of Education* in 1954 a whole slew of other political issues have fallen into the lap of the Court—affirmative action, abortion, gay rights—issues that touch a sensitive chord in multiethnic, multicultural America. This, together with the increasing ability of national interest groups associated with these issues to promote their objectives in federal court, has meant that the judiciary has had to address these extremely explosive issues whether it wants to or not, as seen with the prolonged reaction to the Court's 1973 *Roe v. Wade* decision legalizing abortion. We have also seen other instances where Congress has passed legislation of obviously dubious constitutionality to cater to ephemeral national sentiments—flag desecration and the line-item veto come to mind—fairly secure in the knowledge that the Court will take the political opprobrium for rejecting them. Aside from the obvious concerns for the integrity of the electoral process if the least electorally accountable branch of the federal government is making more and more significant decisions, "buck passing" to the judiciary has also been unhealthy for the Court and for the relationship between the branches.

Naturally, as the Court becomes embroiled in an ever-widening range of policy questions, the stakes regarding who actually sits on the High Bench get much higher. Prior to 1968 only one Supreme Court nominee in this century—Judge John Parker in 1930—had been rejected by the Senate, and nominations for the lower federal courts were invariably rubber-stamped by the Senate, even when that body and the presidency were controlled by different parties. Since 1968 (coinciding with the ideological assertiveness of the late Warren Court) five nominees to the Supreme Court have been rejected by the Senate or withdrawn, and during the Clinton administration, even appointments to federal district and circuit courts have been bitterly contested by the Republican majority in the Senate, as outlined in O'Brien's chapter. We can expect no less opposition and obstruction from Democratic senators to the appointees of the next Republican president. Of course, the ultimate example of the politicization of the judicial nominating process was the grisly spectacle of the confirmation hearings for Supreme Court Justice Clarence Thomas in 1992. The stakes in judicial nominations have gotten so high for interest groups and members of Congress with issues before the Court that any tactic is seen as legitimate to derail a nominee whose initial appointment was driven by a desire by opposing interests to get a more favorable balance of power among the nine justices. In such an atmosphere it is legitimate to ask whether a Republican Senate could have confirmed President Clinton's eminently well-qualified and politically moderate nominees, Ruth Bader Ginsburg and Stephen Breyer.

The issue of congressional redistricting is an instance where Congress and the Court have gotten desperately entangled since justices first pronounced on malapportionment in *Baker v. Carr* (1962). Justice Frankfurter's fear in his dissent that this decision would mire the Court in political conflict has been fully corroborated. Since *Baker v. Carr*, followed by the Voting Rights Act of 1965 and its subsequent amendments, the Court has found other reasons to involve itself in district drawing: for reasons of partisanship (*Davis v. Bandemer* 1986), shape, and contiguity (*Shaw v. Reno* 1993). Of course, opening up new avenues for litigation in the redistricting process merely encouraged the parties involved to increasingly resort to the Court for resolution, so that in the 1990s many states' congressional and state redistricting plans were drawn by federal judges or their designees. As a consequence of judicial rulings, districts have been drawn and redrawn two to four times in the states of Georgia and North Carolina since 1990. For the 2000 census, as Brunell's essay illustrates, federal court intervention has even been drawn into the means of conducting the decennial census on which the entire apportionment and redistricting process is based.

Another area of judicial encroachment into legislative authority not dealt with in this volume is the use of concerted lawsuits and settlements in state courts to drive a change in national policy. This has already been accomplished with some success by anti-smoking and public health groups in forcing a massive legal settlement with policy implications on the tobacco industry and a similar approach is being attempted by anti-gun forces and politicians toward arms manufacturers. Again, we may ask to what extent should state juries and judges set national policy on such politically significant areas, and does this pose a threat to democratic values?

As we begin the new century, then, Congress and the Court have extended their "ongoing conversation" to an ever-wider scope of policy issues. While we can—with some legitimacy—criticize the system as lacking the "democratic" values it claims to espouse by giving so much political power to an unelected judiciary, we should remember that the framers of the Constitution of the United States did not intend it to establish a "democratic" government in the modern sense of the term. Indeed, their separation of powers was precisely intended to preclude the national government from bending too easily to the popular will. Moreover, while the process of making change in public policy in the United States is prolonged, messy, and regularly gridlocked, the course of U.S. history appears to indicate that Finley Peter Dunne's Mr. Dooley was probably right: the Supreme Court does ultimately follow election returns (O'Brien 1986, 295). Somehow a wide public consensus on policy change or opposition to it will be reflected even in the jurisprudence of the unelected judicial branch. As Fisher's chapter so well illustrates, when Congress, the presidency, or the judiciary oversteps the constraints on its power, the other branches will check it.

How does an unelected judicial branch ultimately reflect the public consensus? Presidents will seek to appoint judges who reflect their views, and in an age of increasing legislative activity by the Court, they will pay even closer attention to who those nominees are. In the confirmation process the Senate will likely accept presidential nominees who are in the "mainstream" of public opinion and be far more reluctant to confirm those who diverge dramatically. If the Court is defying the public will on major questions of the day then the branches that are more responsive to that will can, through the replacement of justices, bend the Court to their direction. There may be time lags, but ultimately the new political majority will be reflected at the judicial level as well. From the Court's perspective responsiveness to electoral trends also makes strategic sense because lacking the means to enforce its decisions, what power the Court possesses is contingent upon its authority and legitimacy with the broader public.

The events of 1935 to 1945 provide a clear example of how the Court eventually becomes responsive to deep political change. After striking down a major portion of the New Deal economic program in 1935, the Court saw that program endorsed by overwhelming majorities in the 1936 Democratic landslide, and the reelected Franklin D. Roosevelt, urged Congress to make dramatic changes in the composition of the Court to reflect that popular consensus. The

Supreme Court backed off and Roosevelt's plan was shelved, and by the time of his death in 1945 the Court was composed entirely of New Deal supporters. Ultimately the Supreme Court did follow the election returns. Similarly, when the Warren and Burger courts overstepped the mark with their dramatically liberal jurisprudence in the late 1960s and early 1970s, nominations, confirmations, and replacements produced the more conservative later Burger and Rehnquist courts.

One final observation on Congress and the Court that is worthy of mentionis the remarkable institutional conservatism of both branches. Despite Congress's sweeping constitutional powers to alter the structure of the Supreme Court, that structure has remained more or less unchanged for over a century. Even though the workload of the Court has increased so dramatically, the number of justices appears to be permanently stuck at one panel of nine members. The constitutional strictures on life-tenure are also unquestioned although constitutional courts in other advanced liberal democracies function well with term limitations. A more constant rotation of personnel might actually help to "depoliticize" judicial nominations and make the Court more responsive to change in legal thinking and public policy by bringing in "fresh blood" on a regular basis. Unlike the other branches the Court is highly resistant to television coverage, perhaps to guard the relative anonymity and "judicial mystique" that are such critical components of its authority.

Turning our attention to the legislative branch we might also mention Congress's disinclination to question the plurality, single-member district system for electing the U.S. House, although the recent history of congressional redistricting and Brunell's chapter would appear to indicate that this method is singularly inappropriate for a diverse, multiethnic society. The districts (the total number, 435, has stayed the same since 1910 despite massive population growth) are too large (now with over half a million voters) for members to effectively represent constituents. Moreover, the redrawing of districts to ensure the representation of minorities has led to political turmoil in the redistricting process—a situation where most districts are so safe for either party that there is no real electoral competition. On a national scale this has also led to the congressional parties being far too beholden to committed minorities of their own partisans in safe seats. Despite these obvious flaws President Clinton's nomination of Professor Lani Guinier for the post of Assistant Attorney General for Civil Rights in 1993 was rejected primarily due to academic articles she had published, suggesting possible alternative means for improving the representation of minorities in the House of Representatives. The tenacity of the seniority system—although much weakened over the past thirty years—is another mark of Congress's institutional conservatism. The U.S. Senate has a whole set of oddities of its own that prove remarkably resistant to change or reform, beginning with its constitutionally guaranteed malapportionment, but also including practices such as the filibuster, holds, and non-germane floor amendments.

So these very conservative institutions make policymakers jump through an extraordinary number of political hoops to effect major political change. Yet when the conditions are ripe the system can move with alarming speed as soon as an overwhelming national consensus presents itself. None of the niceties of judicial review or the Bill of Rights precluded *Plessey v. Ferguson* (1896); the Prohibition amendment and the Volstead Act; and *Korematsu v. United States* (1944), the incarceration of Japanese Americans during World War II. So while the struggle or conversation between Congress and the Court over the legislative power has served to check the overweening ambitions of either branch in a fashion that has been healthy for American democracy, both are ultimately powerless to resist powerful demands for political change coming from the wider society. Each branch has been at its best, however, in at least compelling serious reconsideration of those demands before they are translated into policy outcomes that may have serious consequences for the freedoms of American citizens and the social stability of American society and the body politic.

Bibliography

BOOKS AND ARTICLES

Abraham, Henry J. 1998. *The Judicial Process.* New York: Oxford University Press.

Alliance for Justice. 1999. Judicial Selection Project Annual Report. <http://www.afj.org/jsp/index.html>.

Anderson, Edward F. 1996. *Peyote: The Divine Cactus.* 2d ed. Tucson: University of Arizona Press.

Anderson, Margo J. 1988. *The American Census: A Social History.* New Haven: Yale University Press.

Anderson, Margo J., and Stephen E. Fienberg. 1999. *Who Counts? The Politics of Census-Taking in Contemporary America.* New York: Russell Sage Foundation.

Baker, Leonard. 1974. *John Marshall: A Life in Law.* New York: Macmillan.

Banks, Christopher P. 1999. "Reversals of Precedent and Judicial Policy-Making: How Judicial Conceptions of *Stare Decisis* in the U.S. Supreme Court Influence Social Change." *Akron Law Review* 32: 1–25. <http://web.lexis-nexis.com>.

Basler, Roy P., ed. 1953. *Collected Works of Abraham Lincoln.* 9 vols. New Brunswick, N.J.: Rutgers University Press.

Baum, Lawrence. 1992. *The Supreme Court,* 4th ed. Washington, D.C.: CQ Press.

———. 1997. *The Puzzle of Judicial Behavior.* Ann Arbor: University of Michigan Press.

———. 1998. *The Supreme Court,* 6th ed. Washington, D.C.: CQ Press.

Berger, Raoul. 1969. *Congress v. the Supreme Court.* Cambridge: Harvard University Press.

———. 1974. *Impeachment: The Constitutional Problems.* Cambridge: Harvard University Press.

Beveridge, Albert J. 1919. *The Life of John Marshall.* 4 vols. New York: Houghton Mifflin.

Biskupic, Joan, and Elder Witt. 1997. *Guide to the Supreme Court*, 3d ed. 2 vols. Washington, D.C.: CQ Press.

Blasi, Vincent, ed. 1983. *The Burger Court: The Counter-Revolution That Wasn't*. New Haven: Yale University Press.

Blondel, Jean. 1995. *Comparative Government: An Introduction*. London: Prentice-Hall–Harvester Wheatsheaf.

Bork, Robert H. 1990. *The Tempting of America: The Political Seduction of Law*. New York: Free Press.

Breckenridge, Adam C. 1970. *Congress Against the Court*. Lincoln: University of Nebraska Press.

Breiman, Leo. 1994. "The 1991 Census Adjustment: Undercount or Bad Data?" *Statistical Science* 9: 458–537.

Brest, Paul. 1986. "Congress as Constitutional Decisionmaker and Its Power to Counter Judicial Doctrine." *Georgia Law Review* 21: 57–106.

Brigham, John. 1987. *The Cult of the Court*. Philadelphia: Temple University Press.

Brown, Lawrence D., Morris L. Eaton, David A. Freedman, Stephen P. Klein, Richard A. Olshen, Kenneth W. Wachter, Martin T. Wells, and Donald Ylvisaker. 1999. *Statistical Controversies in Census 2000*. Technical Report 537, Department of Statistics. Berkeley: University of California Press.

Brunell, Thomas L. Forthcoming. "Redistricting in the Aughts: The Impact of a Two-Number Census." *American Review of Politics*.

———. 2000. "Using Statistical Sampling to Estimate the U.S. Population: The Methodological and Political Debate over Census 2000." *PS* 33.

Burger, Warren E. 1985. "The Doctrine of Judicial Review: Mr. Marshall, Mr. Jefferson, and Mr. Marbury." In *Views from the Bench: The Judiciary and Constitutional Politics*, edited by Mark W. Cannon and David M. O'Brien. Chatham, N.J.: Chatham House.

Bushnell, Eleanore. 1992. *Crimes, Follies and Misfortunes: The Federal Impeachment Trials*. Urbana: University of Illinois Press.

Cappelletti, Mauro. 1983. "Who Watches the Watchmen: A Comparative Study on Judicial Responsibility." *American Journal of Comparative Law* 31: 1–62.

Carp, Robert A., Donald Songer, C. K. Rowland, Ronald Stidham, and Lisa Richey-Tracy. 1993. "The Voting Behavior of Judges Appointed by President Bush." *Judicature* 76 (April): 298–302.

Carter, Stephen L. 1986. "The Morgan Power and the Forced Reconsideration of Constitutional Decisions." *University of Chicago Law Review* 53: 824–65.

Casper, Gerhard. 1976. "Constitutional Constraints on the Conduct of Foreign and Defense Policy: A Nonjudicial Model." *University of Chicago Law Review* 43: 463.

Choper, Jesse H. 1982. "Congressional Power to Expand Judicial Definitions of the Substantive Terms of the Civil War Amendments." *Minnesota Law Review* 67: 299–341.

———. 1998. "On the Difference in Importance between Supreme Court Doctrine and Actual Consequences: A Review of the Supreme Court's 1996–1997 Term." *Cardozo Law Review* 19: 2259–69.

Clayton, Cornell. 1999. "Law, Politics, and the Rehnquist Court: Structural Influences on Supreme Court Decision Making." In *The Supreme Court in American Politics*, edited by Howard Gillman and Cornell Clayton. Lawrence: University Press of Kansas.

Congressional Record. 1878. 45th Cong., 2d sess., Vol. 7, pt. 2.

Congressional Record. 1879. 45th Cong., 3d sess., Vol. 8, pt. 2.

Congressional Record. 1890. 51st Cong., 1st sess., Vol. 21, pt. 5.

Congressional Record. 1955. 84th Cong., 1st sess., Vol. 101, pt. 1.

Congressional Record. 1958. 85th Cong., 2d sess., Vol. 104, pt. 11.

Congressional Record. 1970. 91st Cong., 2d sess., Vol. 116, pt. 31.

Congressional Record. 1978. 95th Cong., 2d sess., Vol. 124, pt. 25.

Davis, Sue. 1989. *Justice Rehnquist and the Constitution.* Princeton, N.J.: Princeton University Press.

Davidson, Roger H. 1988. "What Judges Ought to Know about Lawmaking in Congress." In *Judges and Legislators: Toward Institutional Comity,* edited by Robert A. Katzmann. Washington, D.C.: Brookings.

Davidson, Roger H., and Colton C. Campbell. Forthcoming. "The Senate and the Executive." In *Esteemed Colleagues: Civility and Deliberation in the United States Senate,* edited by Burdett A. Loomis. Washington, D.C.: Brookings.

Day, Chris. 1991. "*Employment Division v. Smith:* Free Exercise Clause Loses Balance on Peyote." *Baylor Law Review* 43: 577–608.

De Figueiredo, John M., and Emerson H. Tiller. 1996. "Congressional Control of the Courts: A Theoretical and Empirical Analysis of Expansion of the Federal Judiciary." *The Journal of Law and Economics* 39: 435–62.

Derthick, Martha. 2000. "American Federalism: Half-Full or Half-Empty?" *The Brookings Review* (Winter): 24–27.

Ducat, Craig R. 2000. *Constitutional Interpretation,* 7th ed. Belmont, Calif.: Wadsworth.

Durbin, Thomas M. 1996. *Congressional Majority-Minority Redistricting.* Report No. 96-665 A. Washington, D.C.: Congressional Research Service.

Edsall, Thomas Byrne, and Mary Edsall. 1991. *The Impact of Race, Rights, and Taxes on American Politics.* New York: Norton.

Epstein, Lee, and Jack Knight. 1998. *The Choices Justices Make.* Washington, D.C.: CQ Press.

Eskridge, William N., Jr. 1991. "Overriding Supreme Court Statutory Interpretation Decisions." *Yale Law Journal* 101: 331–455.

Farrand, Max, ed. 1937. *The Records of the Federal Convention of 1787.* 4 vols. New Haven: Yale University Press.

Fisher, Louis. 1997. *Constitutional Conflicts between Congress and the President,* 4th ed., revised. Lawrence: University Press of Kansas.

———. 2001. American Constitutional Law. 4th ed. Durham, N.C.: Carolina Academic Press.

Foster, James C., and Susan M. Leeson. 1998. *Constitutional Law: Cases in Context,* vol. 1., Upper Saddle River, N.J.: Prentice Hall.

Freedman, Max. 1967. *Roosevelt and Frankfurter: Their Correspondence.* Boston: Little, Brown.

Fried, Charles. 1995. "The Supreme Court, 1994 Term—Foreword: Revolutions?" *Harvard Law Review* 109: 13–73.

Gerhardt, Michael. 1996. *The Federal Impeachment Process*. Princeton, N.J.: Princeton University Press.

Glennon, Michael J. 1984. "The Use of Custom in Resolving Separation of Power Disputes." *Boston University Law Review* 64: 109.

Goldman, Sheldon. 1993. "Bush's Judicial Legacy: The Final Imprint." *Judicature* 76 (April): 282–97.

———. 1997. *Picking Federal Judges: Lower Court Selection from Roosevelt Through Reagan*. New Haven: Yale University Press.

Gordon, James D. 1991. "Free Exercise on the Mountaintop." *California Law Review* 97: 91–116.

Greenhouse, Linda. 1999. "High Court Faces Moment of Truth in Federalism Cases." *New York Times*, March 28, 23.

Green, John C., and Daniel Shea, eds. 1999. *The State of the Parties*. 3d ed. Lanham, Md.: Rowman & Littlefield.

Greve, Michael S. 1999. *Real Federalism: Why It Matters, How It Could Happen*. Washington, D.C.: American Enterprise Institute.

Gunther, Gerald. 1984. "Congressional Power to Curtail Federal Court Jurisdiction: An Opinionated Guide to the Ongoing Debate." *Stanford Law Review* 36(4): 895–922.

Hamilton, Alexander, James Madison, and John Jay, eds., with introduction by Garry Wills. 1982. *The Federalist Papers*. Toronto: Bantam.

Hix, Simon. 1999. *The Political System of the European Union*. Houndsmills: Macmillan.

Hogan, Howard. 1993. The 1990 Post-Enumeration Survey: Operations and Results. *Journal of the American Statistical Association*. September, 88 (423): 1047–60.

———. 2000. "Accuracy and Coverage Evaluation: Theory and Application." Presented at the 2000 DSE Workshop of the National Academy of Science Panel to Review the 2000 Census, 2–3 February.

Horn, Constance. 1993. "The Politics of Presidential Appointment: The Old and New Culture of Job Seeking in Washington." *Impressions*. 4 (September/October): 20–24.

Ignagni, Joseph, and James Meernik. 1994. "Explaining Congressional Attempts to Reverse Supreme Court Decisions." *Political Research Quarterly* 47 (June): 353–71.

Jackson, Robert H. 1953. "Maintaining Our Freedoms: The Role of the Judiciary." Delivered to the American Bar Association. Boston, Mass., August 24, 1953; reprinted in *Vital Speeches*. No. 24, Vol. XIX, p. 761 (October 1).

Jacobson, Gary C. 1991. *The Electoral Origins of Divided Government*. Boulder, Colo.: Westview.

Katzmann, Robert A. 1997. *Courts & Congress*. Washington, D.C.: Brookings.

Kay, Kenneth R. 1981. "Limiting Federal Court Jurisdiction: The Unforeseen Impact on Courts and Congress." *Judicature* 65 (October): 185–89.

Krutz, Glen S., Richard Fleisher, and Jon Bond. 1998. "From Abe Fortas to Zoe Baird: Why Some Presidential Nominations Fail in the Senate." *American Political Science Review* 92(4): 871–81.

Landes, William M., and Richard A. Posner. 1975. "The Independent Judiciary in an Interest-Group Perspective." *Journal of Law and Economics* 18: 875–905.

Laycock, Douglas. 1993. "The Supreme Court's Assault on Free Exercise and the Amicus Brief That Was Never Filed." *Journal of Law and Religion* 8: 99–114.

———. 1995. "RFRA, Congress, and the Ratchet." *Montana Law Review* 56: 145–70.

Lewis, Neil A. 1997. "Clinton Has a Chance to Shape the Courts." *New York Times,* February 9, 16.

Light, Paul C. 2000. "Appointees on the Barbie." *Government Executive* (May): 96.

Mackenzie, G. Calvin, and Robert Shogan. 1996. "The Presidential Appointment Process: Historical Development, Contemporary Operations, Current Issues." In *Obstacle Course: The Report of the Twentieth Century Fund Task Force on the Presidential Appointment Process.* New York: Twentieth Century Fund Press.

Marin, Kenneth. 1991. "*Employment Division v. Smith:* The Supreme Court Alters the State of the Free Exercise Doctrine." *American University Law Review* 40: 1431–76.

McConnell, Michael. 1991. "Should Congress Pass Legislation Restoring the Broader Interpretation of the Free Exercise of Religion?" *Harvard Journal of Law and Public Policy* 15: 189–213.

———. 1995. "Accommodation of Religion." *Supreme Court Review* 1: 1–59.

McDonald, Forrest. 1992. "Tenth Amendment." In *The Oxford Companion to the Supreme Court of the United States,* ed. Kermith L. Hall. New York: Oxford University Press.

Meese, Edwin. 1985. "The Attorney General's View of the Supreme Court: Toward Jurisprudence of Original Intention." In *Law and Public Affairs, Special Issue, Public Administration Review,* edited by Charles Wise and David M. O'Brien. 45 (1985): 701–704.

Mény, Yves, and Andrew Knapp. 1998. *Government and Politics in Western Europe.* Oxford: Oxford University Press.

Mikva, Abner J., and Jeff Bleich. 1991. "When Congress Overrules the Court." *California Law Review* 79: 729–50.

Murphy, Walter F. 1962. *Congress and the Court: A Case Study in the American Political Process.* Chicago: University of Chicago Press.

Nagel, Stuart S. 1962 [1973]. "Court-Curbing Periods in American History." In *The Impact of Supreme Court Decisions,* edited by Theodore Becker and Malcolm Feeley. Oxford: Oxford University Press.

O'Brien, David M. 1986. *Storm Center.* New York: Norton.

———. 1987. "The Supreme Court from Warren to Burger to Rehnquist." *PS* 20: 12–20.

———. 1988. "The Reagan Judges: His Most Enduring Legacy." In *The Reagan Legacy: Promise and Performance,* edited by Charles O. Jones. Chatham, N.J.: Chatham House.

———. 1989a. "Filling Justice William O. Douglas's Seat: President Gerald R. Ford's Appointment of Associate Justice John Paul Stevens." In *Yearbook of the Supreme Court Historical Society—1989.* Washington, D.C.: Supreme Court Historical Society.

———. 1989b. "Federalism as a Metaphor in the Constitutional Politics of Public Administration." *Public Administration Review* 49: 411–19.

———. 1993. "The Rehnquist Court and Federal Preemption: In Search of a Theory." *Publius* 23: 1–14.

———. 1995. "Judicial Review." In *The Encyclopedia of the United States Congress,* Vol. 3, edited by Ronald C. Bacon, Roger H. Davidson, and Morton Keller. New York: Simon & Schuster.

———. 1996. "Charting the Rehnquist Court's Course: How the Center Folds, Holds, and Shifts." *New York Law School Law Review* 40: 981–98.

———. 1998. *Judicial Roulette.* New York: Twentieth Century Fund Press.

———. 2000a. *Supreme Court Watch 1999.* New York: Norton.

———. 2000b. *Constitutional Law and Politics, Vol. 1, Struggles for Power and Governmental Accountability,* 4th ed. New York: Norton.

———. 2000c. *Constitutional Law and Politics, Vol. 2, Civil Rights and Civil Liberties,* 4th ed. New York: Norton.

———. 2000d. "Judicial Legacies: The Clinton Presidency and the Courts." In *The Clinton Legacy,* edited by Colin Campbell and Bert A. Rockman. Chatham, N.J.: Chatham House.

———. 2000e. *Storm Center: The Supreme Court in American Politics,* 5th ed. New York: Norton.

Opinions of the Attorneys General of the United States. 1868. Washington, D.C.: W. H. & O. H. Morrison.

Peterson, Mark A. 1998. "The President and Congress." In *The Presidency and the Political System,* 5th ed., edited by Michael Nelson. Washington, D.C.: CQ Press.

Phillips, Kevin P. 1970. *The Emerging Republican Majority.* New York: Anchor.

Pope, Charles. 1999. "Supreme Court Ruling Offers Little Hope for Ending Census Sampling Debate." *CQ Weekly Report.* 30 January: 259–60.

Powell, H. Jefferson. 1982. "The Compleat Jeffersonian: Justice Rehnquist and Federalism." *Yale Law Journal* 91: 1317–70.

Pritchett, C. Herman. 1961. *Congress Versus the Supreme Court.* Minneapolis: University of Minnesota Press.

Rae, Nicol C. 1989. *The Decline and Fall of Liberal Republicans: From 1952 to Present.* New York: Oxford University Press.

Ramseyer, J. Mark. 1994. "Puzzling (In)Dependence of Courts: A Comparative Approach." *Journal of Legal Studies* 23: 721–48.

Rawlings, Tom C. 1995. "*Employment Division, Dept. of Human Resources v. Smith:* The Supreme Court Deserts the Free Exercise Clause." *Georgia Law Review* 25: 567–93.

Rehnquist, William H., Chief Justice. 1992. *Grand Inquests: The Historic Impeachments of Justice Samuel Chase and President Andrew Johnson.* New York: Morrow.

———. 1999. "The 1998 Year-End Report of the Federal Judiciary." *The Third Branch.* Washington, D.C.

Report of the Committee on Adjustment of Postcensal Estimates, Bureau of the Census. 1992. "Assessment of Accuracy of Adjusted Versus Unadjusted 1990 Census Base for Use in Intercensal Estimates." 7 August, Washington, D.C.

Rice, Charles E. 1981. "Limiting Federal Court Jurisdiction: The Constitutional Basis for the Proposals in Congress Today." *Judicature* 65 (October): 190–97.

Richardson, James D. 1897. *A Compilation of the Messages and Papers of the Presidents.* 20 vols. New York: Bureau of National Literature.

Rohde, David W. 1991. *Parties and Leaders in the Postreform House.* Chicago: University of Chicago Press.

Rossum, Ralph A. 1983. "Congress, the Constitution, and the Appellate Jurisdiction of the Supreme Court: The Letter and the Spirit of the Exceptions Clause." *William and Mary Law Review* 24(3): 385–428.

Rutkus, Denis Steven. 1993. *The Supreme Court Appointment Process: Should It Be Reformed?* Congressional Research Service Report No. 93-290. Washington, D.C.

———. 1994. *Senate Judiciary Committee Consideration of Supreme Court Nominations.* Congressional Research Service No. 94-479 GOV. Washington, D.C.

Scharpf, Fritz W. 1997. *Games Real Actors Play: Actor-Centered Institutionalism in Policy Research.* Boulder, Colo.: Westview.

Scheiber, Harry N. 1992. "Federalism." In *The Oxford Companion to the Supreme Court of the United States*, edited by Kermith L. Hall. New York: Oxford University Press.

Schmidhauser, John R., and Larry L. Berg. 1972. *The Supreme Court and Congress: Conflict and Interaction, 1945–1968.* New York: Free Press.

Schwartz, Bernard. 1983. *Super Chief: Earl Warren and His Supreme Court—A Judicial Biography.* New York: New York University Press.

Segal, Jeffrey A. 1997. "Separation-of-Powers Games in the Positive Theory of Congress and Courts." *American Political Science Review* 91 (March): 28–44.

Segal, Jeffrey A., and Harold J. Spaeth. 1993. *The Supreme Court and the Attitudinal Model.* New York: Cambridge University Press.

Shapiro, David L. 1976. "Mr. Justice Rehnquist: A Preliminary View." *Harvard Law Review* 90: 293–357.

Silverstein, Mark. 1994. *Judicious Choices: The New Politics of Supreme Court Confirmations.* New York: Norton.

Sinclair, Barbara. 1995. *Legislators, Leaders, and Lawmaking: The U.S. House of Representatives in the Post-Reform Era.* Baltimore: Johns Hopkins University Press.

———. 1997. *Unorthodox Lawmaking: New Legislative Processes in the U.S. Congress*, 1st ed. Washington, D.C.: CQ Press.

Smith, Jean Edward. 1996. *John Marshall: Definer of a Nation.* New York: Holt.

Solimine, Michael E., and James L. Walker. 1992. "The Next Word: Congressional Response to Supreme Court Statutory Decisions." *Temple Law Review* 65: 425–58.

Stark, P. B. 1999. *Differences Between the 1990 and 2000 Census Adjustment Plans, and Their Impact on Error.* Technical Report 550, Department of Statistics. Berkeley: University of California Press.

Stewart, Omer C. 1987. *Peyote Religion: A History.* Norman: University of Oklahoma Press.

Stumpf, Harry P. 1965. "Congressional Response to Supreme Court Rulings: The Interaction of Law and Politics." *Journal of Public Law* 14 (November): 392–95.

Stone Sweet, Alec. 2000. *Governing with Judges: Constitutional Politics in Europe.* New York: Oxford University Press.

Tate, C. Neal, and Torbjorn Vallinder, eds. 1995. *The Global Expansion of Judicial Power.* New York: New York University Press.

Ten Broek, Jacobus. 1939. "Partisan Politics and Federal Judgeship Impeachment Since 1903." *Minnesota Law Review* 23: 185–204.

Titus, Herbert W. 1995. "The Free Exercise Clause: Past, Present, and Future." *Regent University Law Review* 6: 7–63.

Toma, Eugenia F. 1991. "Congressional Influence and the Supreme Court: The Budget as a Signaling Device." *Journal of Legal Studies* 20: 131–46.

Tushnet, Mark. 1999. "Foreword: The New Constitutional Order and the Chastening of Constitutional Aspiration." *Harvard Law Review* 113: 29–109.

Tushnet, Mark, ed. 1993. *The Warren Court in Historical and Political Perspective.* Charlottesville: University Press of Virginia.

U.S. Congress. House. Committee on the Judiciary, Subcommittee on Civil and Constitutional Rights. 1990. *Religious Freedom Restoration Act of 1990.* 101st Cong., 2d sess., 27 September.

U.S. Congress. House. Committee on the Judiciary, Subcommittee on Civil and Constitutional Rights. 1992. *Religious Freedom Restoration Act of 1991.* 102nd Cong., 2d sess., 13–14 May.

U.S. Congress. Senate. Committee on the Judiciary. 1993. *Religious Freedom Restoration Act of 1992.* 102d Cong., 2d sess., 18 September.

U.S. Congress. Joint. Committee on the Organization of Congress. 1993. *Interbranch Relations.* 103rd Cong., 1st sess., 22, 24, 29 June.

Van Tassel, Emily Field. 1993. *Why Judges Resign: Influences on Federal Judicial Service, 1789-1992.* Washington, D.C.: Federal Judicial History Office, Federal Judicial Center.

Volcansek, Mary L. 1993. *Judicial Impeachment: None Called for Justice.* Urbana: University of Illinois Press.

Volcansek, Mary L., Elisabetta de Franciscis, and Jacqueline Lucienne Lafon. 1996. *Judicial Misconduct: A Cross-National Comparison.* Gainesville: University Press of Florida.

Waite, Preston Jay, and Howard Hogan. 1998. *Statistical Methodologies for Census 2000.* Typescript. U.S. Bureau of the Census.

Warren, Earl. 1962. "The Bill of Rights and the Military." *New York University Law Review* 37: 193.

Weaver, R. Kent, and Bert A. Rockman. 1993. "Assessing the Effects of Institutions." In *Do Institutions Matter? Government Capabilities in the United States and Abroad,* edited by Bert A. Rockman and R. Kent Weaver. Washington, D.C.: Brookings.

Weingast, Barry R. 1996. "Political Institutions: Rational Choice Perspectives." In *A New Handbook of Political Science,* edited by Robert E. Goodin and Hans-Dieter Klingeman. Oxford: Oxford University Press.

Wilkinson, J. Harvie, III. 1999. "Fear of Federalism." *Washington Post,* November 26, A45.

Yarwood, Dean L., and Bradley C. Canon. 1980. "On the Supreme Court's Annual Trek to the Capitol." *Judicature* 63 (February): 322–27.

CASES

Adair v. United States, 208 U.S. 161 (1908).
Adams Fruit Co. v. Barrett, 494 U.S. 638 (1990).
Adarand Constructors v. Pena, 515 U.S. 200 (1995).
Adkins v. Children's Hospital, 261, U.S. 525 (1923).
A.L.A. Schechter Poultry Corp. v. United States, 295 U.S. 495 (1935).
Alden v. Maine, 119 S.Ct. 2240 (1999).
Bailey v. Drexel Furniture Co., 259 U.S. 20 (1922).

Baker v. Carr, 369 U.S. 186 (1962).

Black v. Employment Division, 301 Or. 221 (1986).

Boerne v. Flores, 521 U.S. 507 (1997).

Bradwell v. State, 83 U.S. 130 (1873).

Brown v. Allen, 344 U.S. 443 (1953).

Brown v. Board of Education, 347 U.S. 483 (1954).

Brzonkala v. Morrison, 169 F.3d 820 (4th Cir., 1999).

Buckley v. Valeo, 424 U.S. 1 (1976).

Champion v. Ames, 188 U.S. 321 (1903).

Chisholm v. Georgia, 2 Dall. 419 (1793).

City of Boerne v. Flores, 521 U.S. 507 (1997).

City of Richmond v. J.A. Croson, 488 U.S. 469 (1989).

Clinton v. City of New York, 118 S.Ct. 2091 (1998).

Clinton v. Glavin, 525 U.S. 959 (1998).

Clinton v. Jones, 117 S.Ct. 1636 (1997).

Colegrove v. Green, 328 U.S. 549 (1946).

College Savings Bank v. Florida, 527 U.S. (1999).

Cooper v. Aaron, 358 U.S. 1 (1958).

Coppage v. Kansas, 236 U.S. 1 (1915).

Crosby v. National Foreign Trade Council, 120 S.Ct. 2288 (2000).

Davis v. Bandemer, 478 U.S. 106 (1986).

Dellmuth v. Muth, 491 U.S. 223 (1989).

Department of Commerce v. U.S. House of Representatives, 525 U.S. 316 (1999).

Department of Commerce v. U.S. House of Representatives, 119 S.Ct. 765 (1999).

Dred Scott v. Sandford, 60 U.S. 393 (1857).

Duncan v. Louisiana, 391 U.S. 145 (1968).

Employment Division of Oregon v. Smith, 485 U.S. 660 (1988).

Employment Division, Department of Human Resources of Oregon v. Smith, 492 U.S. 872 (1990).

Engel v. Vitale, 370 U.S. 421 (1962).

Florida Prepaid Postsecondary Education Expense Board v. College Savings Bank, 119 S.Ct. 2199 (1999).

Flores v. City of Boerne, 877 F. Supp. 255 (W.D. Tex. 1995).

Flores v. City of Boerne, 73 F. 3d 1352 (5th Cir. 1996).

Freeman v. Pitts, 503 U.S. 467 (1992).

Fry v. United States, 421 U.S. 542 (1975).

Garcia v. San Antonio Metropolitan Transit Authority, 469 U.S. 528 (1985).

Gideon v. Wainwright, 372 U.S. 335 (1963).

Goldman v. Weinberger, 475 U.S. 503 (1986).

Graves v. New York ex rel. O'Keefe, 306 U.S. 466 (1939).

Gregory v. Ashcroft, 501 U.S. 452 (1991).

Griswold v. Connecticut, 381 U.S. 479 (1965).

Hammer v. Dagenhart, 247 U.S. 251 (1918).

Heart of Atlanta Motel v. United States, 379 U.S. 241 (1964).

Helvering v. Griffiths, 318 U.S. 371 (1943).

Hentoff v. Ichord, 318 F. Supp. 1175 (D.D.C. 1970).

Hirabayashi v. United States, 320 U.S. 81 (1943).

Hubbard v. United States, 514 U.S. 695 (1995).

Immigration and Naturalization Service v. Chadha, 462 U.S. 919 (1983).

Inland Waterways Corp. v. Young, 309 U.S. 517 (1940).

Jacobson v. Massachusetts, 197 U.S. 11 (1905).

Jencks v. United States, 353 U.S. 657 (1957).

John Hancock Mutual Life Insurance Co. v. Harris Bank, 510 U.S. 927 (1993).

Karcher v. Daggett, 462 U.S. 725, 738 (1983).

Katzenbach v. Morgan, 384 U.S. 641 (1966).

Kimel v. Florida Board of Regents, 120 S.Ct. 631 (2000).

Korematsu v. United States, 323 U.S. 214 (1944).

Leisy v. Hardin, 135 U.S. 100 (1890).

Lochner v. New York, 198 U.S. 45 (1905).

Lynce v. Mathis, 137 L. Ed. 2d 63 (1997).

Lyng v. Northwest Cemetery Association, 485 U.S. 439 (1989).

Marbury v. Madison, 1 Cr. (5 U.S.) 137 (1803).

Maryland v. Wirtz, 392 U.S. 183 (1968).

McCray v. United States, 195 U.S. 27 (1904).

McCulloch v. Maryland, 4 Wheat. 316 (1819).

Mississippi University for Women v. Hogan, 458 U.S. 718 (1982).

Morrison v. Olson, 487 U.S. 654 (1988).

Muller v. Oregon, 208 U.S. 412 (1908).

National Labor Relations Board v. Jones & Laughlin Steel Corporation, 301 U.S. 1 (1937).

National League of Cities v. Usery, 426 U.S. 833 (1976).

New York v. United States, 505 U.S. 144 (1992).

Niemotko v. Maryland, 340 U.S. 268 (1951).

O'Lone v. Estate of Shabazz, 482 U.S. 342 (1987).

Pennsylvania v. Nelson, 350 U.S. 497 (1956).

Planned Parenthood of Southeastern Pennsylvania v. Casey, 505 U.S. 833 (1992).

Plessy v. Ferguson, 163 U.S. 537 (1896).

Pollock v. Farmers' Loan and Trust Co., 158 U.S. 601 (1895).

Powell v. McCormack, 395 U.S. 486 (1969).

Primate Protection League v. Administrators of Tulane Educational Fund, 500 U.S. 72 (1991).

Printz v. United States and *Mack v. United States,* 117 S.Ct. 2365 (1997).

Prudential Ins. Co. v. Benjamin, 328 U.S. 408 (1946).

Pulliam v. Allen, 466 U.S. 522 (1984).

Rahrer, In re, 140 U.S. 545 (1891).

Regents of the University of California v. Bakke, 438 U.S. 265 (1978).

Reno v. ACLU, 521 U.S. 844 (1997).

Reno v. Condon, 120 S.Ct. 666 (2000).

Roe v. Wade, 410 U.S. 113 (1973).

Romer v. Evans, 517 U.S. 620 (1996).

significantly 	 ं

Schechter Poultry Corporation v. United States, 295 U.S. 495 (1935).

Seminole Tribe of Florida v. Florida, 517 U.S. 44 (1996).

Senate Select Committee v. Nixon, 498 F.2d 725 (1974).

Shaw v. Reno, 509 U.S 630 (1993).

Sherbert v. Verner, 374 U.S. 398 (1963).

Shurtleff v. United States, 189 U.S. 311 (1903).

Smith v. Employment Division, 75 Or. App. 764 (Or. Ct. App. 1985).

Smith v. Employment Division, 301 Or. 209 (1986).

Smith v. Employment Division of Oregon, 307 Or. 68 (1988).

South Dakota v. Dole, 483 U.S. 203 (1987).

Stuart v. Laird, 5 U.S. 299 (1803).

Swann v. Charlotte-Mecklenberg Board of Education, 401 U.S. 1 (1971).

Texas v. Johnson, 491 U.S. 397 (1989).

United States v. Allocco, 305 F.2d 704 (2d Cir. 1962), cert. denied, 371 U.S. 964 (1963).

United States v. Belmont, 301 U.S. 324 (1937).

United States v. Butler, 297 U.S. 1 (1936).

United States v. Darby, 312 U.S. 100 (1941).

United States v. Eichman, 496 U.S. 310 (1990).

United States v. Locke, 120 S.Ct. 1135 (2000).

United States v. Lopez, 514 U.S. 549 (1995).

United States v. Midwest Oil Co., 236 U.S. 459 (1915).

United States v. Miller, 425 U.S. 435 (1976).

United States v. Morrison, 120 S.Ct. 1740 (2000).

United States v. Nixon, 418 U.S. 683 (1974).

United States v. Woodley, 751 F.2d 1008 (9th Cir. 1985), cert. denied, 475 U.S. 1048 (1986).

Uphaus v. Wyman, 360 U.S. 72 (1959).

U.S. Term Limits, Inc. v. Thornton, 514 U.S. 779 (1995).

Vermont Agency of Natural Resources v. United States ex rel. Stevens, 120 S.Ct. 1858 (2000).

West Coast Hotel v. Parrish, 300 U.S. 379 (1937).

Youngstown Co. v. Sawyer, 343 U.S. 579 (1952).

Zurcher v. Stanford Daily, 436 U.S. 547 (1978).

Index

About the Contributors

THOMAS L. BRUNELL is assistant professor of political science at Binghamton University. His articles appear in the *American Political Science Review, American Journal of Political Science, Journal of Politics,* and *Legislative Studies Quarterly.* He served as an APSA Congressional Fellow in 1998–1999 in the House Subcommittee on the Census.

COLTON C. CAMPBELL is assistant professor of political science at Florida International University, and is currently a visiting assistant professor of political science at American University. He is coeditor of *New Majority or Old Minority? The Impact of Republicans on Congress.* He served as an APSA Congressional Fellow in 1998–1999 in the office of U.S. Senator Bob Graham (D-Fla.).

LOUIS FISHER is senior specialist in American national government at the Congressional Research Service. He is author of numerous books, including *Presidential War Power, American Constitutional Law, The Politics of Shared Power: Congress and the Executive, Constitutional Dialogues: Interpretation as Political Process,* and *Constitutional Conflicts Between Congress and the President.*

CAROLYN N. LONG is assistant professor of political science at Washington State University, Vancouver. She is author of numerous articles on the Supreme Court and religion as well as author of the forthcoming book *Religious Freedom and Indian Rights: The Case of* Oregon v. Smith.

David M. O'Brien is Leone Reaves and George W. Spicer Professor of Government and Foreign Affairs at the University of Virginia. He is author and coauthor of several books, including *Supreme Court Watch* (Annual); *Constitutional Law and Politics* (two vols.); *Struggles for Power and Governmental Accountability and Civil Liberties and Civil Rights*, 2nd ed.; *Storm Center: The Supreme Court in American Politics*, 3rd ed.; *The Politics of American Government*; *The Public's Right to Know: The Supreme Court and the First Amendment; What Process Is Due? Courts and Science-Policy Disputes; Judicial Roulette; Privacy, Law and Public Policy; Abortion and American Politics; The Politics of Technology Assessments;* and *Views from the Bench: The Judiciary and Constitutional Politics*.

Nicol C. Rae is professor of political science at Florida International University. He is author of *The Decline & Fall of the Liberal Republicans: From 1952 to the Present; Southern Democrats, Conservative Reformers: The Freshman Class of the 104th Congress;* and coauthor of *Governing America*. He served as an APSA Congressional Fellow in 1995–96 in the offices of U.S. Senator Thad Cochran (R-Miss.) and U.S. Representative George P. Radanovich (R-Calif.).

John F. Stack Jr. is professor of political science at Florida International University and Director of the Jack D. Gordon Institute for Public Policy and Citizenship. He is author of *International Conflict in an American City: Boston's Irish, Italians, and Jews 1935–1944,* and editor of *Ethnic Identities in a Transnational World; Policy Choices: Critical Issues in American Foreign Policy; The Primordial Challenge: Ethnicity in the Contemporary World;* and *The Ethnic Entanglement*.

Mary L. Volcansek is dean of the Add Ran College of Humanities and Social Sciences at Texas Christian University. She is author and editor of numerous books, including *Judicial Misconduct, Women in Law,* and *Law Above Nations.* She has also written a number of articles and book chapters that examine various aspects of judicial behavior or the roles of courts as political institutions in the United States and in Europe.